# Tales

## of a

# Highland Minister

by

# Rev. Iain Ramsden

## BOOK 1
*(of three)*

## 2nd *Edition*

1

*This book is dedicated to my lovely wife, Jo, for all her help, inspiration and support.*

*I am thankful to family members and a number of good friends for their positivity and encouragement.*

"Tha mi fadah nad chomain"

*'I am very grateful to you'*

# INTRODUCTION

This is the first book in the Trilogy, 'Tales of a Highland Minister' which follow the exploits of the Reverend Colin Campbell, a young Church of Scotland Minister who lived and worked in Glasgow.

Little did he know that travelling to the remote Island of Rhua off the West Coast of Scotland to conduct the funeral service of his maternal Grandmother, would change his life forever.

He fell under the spell of a people and a place where caring and craic, faith, fun and folklore were interwoven like threads of gold and silver, through the fabric of everyday life.

One thing was for sure, life on the Island of Rhua was never going to be dull.

Many of the tales and incidents in this book are taken from personal experience and others may well have happened, but anyone with even the slightest knowledge of the Highlands and Islands of Scotland will recognize the humour and the antics of the local characters – with a dram of poetic license for added flavour.

Set in the late 1940's early 1950's, those of a 'certain age' will readily identify with a simpler way of life. This is a tongue in cheek look at life in those days.

It's been said that Craic and Eccentricity have been superseded by Computers and Electricity but in many areas of the West Coast life is still being lived at a slower pace with wit and wisdom at its heart. It is hoped that you will find both of these within the pages of this book which has been called, "A jewel among the heather."
So, sit back and be transported back to a different time and a very different place.


Gabh Tlachd!
*Enjoy!*

# A bit about the Author

The author is from a small village among the hills in Argyll. and was brought up listening to tales of Scottish folklore, Mythology and ancient stories of banshees, fairies, kelpies, mermaids, otters, seals, witches and much more, at his Highland Grandmother's knee.

His first job after leaving school was on the Ballachulish Ferry. He then upgraded to the Royal Navy, travelling the world at Her Majesty's expense.

After leaving the Royal Navy he went home to Argyll where he worked for a number of years in the Forestry around the West Coast, including Ardrishaig, Lochgilphead, Tarbert (Loch Fyne) as well as Islay and Jura where he acquired a healthy appreciation of the Islay and Jura Malt Whiskies.

In the 1970's he worked as a Navvy on the road between Craignure, Lochdon and Bunessan on the Isle of Mull where he met many old characters from the Highlands as well as a number of charismatic Irish Navvies, many of whom had a treasure chest of stories to tell.

After years of rain, midgies and wood wasps he saw an advert in the Oban Times for Revenue Assistants in HM Customs and Excise, ex Servicemen preferred. Being and ex Serviceman he applied, was accepted and soon began working in and around the Distilleries and Whisky warehouses in the Speyside area.
Poacher turned gamekeeper!

As the years passed he felt an unexpected and yet unshakable 'call' to serve God. This surprised and unsettled him, and after a lengthy conversation with a Minister friend, he applied to the Church of Scotland and was accepted as a Candidate for the Ministry.
He then went to Aberdeen University and 3 years later he Graduated with a Bachelor of Theology Degree. Who would have thought it?

During his final year at university he spent a summer placement on Britain's most remote, inhabited Island, the Island of Foula which is off the West coast of Shetland. It is also known as "The Edge of the World" after a 1913 film and a 1978 BBC documentary about this fascinating and faraway Island.

He was ordained in 1999 and served as a 'Highland Parish Minister' on the Black Isle for 15 years before retiring to Glasgow where, for a further 7 years, he continued his Ministry as Locum in Ferguslie Park, Carntyne, Easterhouse, Erskine and Kilmacolm until finally retiring in 2021.

Although a faithful Minister, the author still keeps a healthy respect for the old traditions and beliefs which were passed on to him by his Highland Grandmother, who now rests in peace in Appin Cemetery.

God certainly does work in mysterious ways!

# CONTENTS

# Chapter 1

*"In the beginning..."*

◆

The Reverend Colin Campbell sat at his desk in Kelvinside, Glasgow, pondering on what his future might hold.

He was a young Ordained Minister of the Church of Scotland who was currently serving as an Assistant Minister in the Barony Church in Glasgow.

He had excelled at University with a 1.1. Bachelor of Arts degree and a 1.1. Bachelor of Divinity degree. If he was ever going to be a contestant on 'Mastermind' his specialised subject would be, 'Ancient Hebrew' (not as much fun as it sounds!).

Colin had always imagined himself living and serving in and around the Glasgow area, working with the poor and the disadvantaged, but this past year or so hadn't turned out as he had hoped. Much of his work had been spent in Admin, Management, Personnel and Planning meetings with other Clergy in and around the Central Belt.

He felt restless and unfulfilled and was thinking about applying to another church where he would be better able to help those in need.

It was a dull Monday morning and he began opening the morning post. He always started by putting the envelopes into two piles, white and brown. He would open the white envelopes first and then reluctantly start on the brown envelopes as these were usually bills or official communications and they could wait.

Among the white envelopes were a mixture of letters and belated cards on his recent birthday, all very mundane.

However, there was something else. In the brown pile, an official-looking envelope with his address neatly typed on it caught his attention. He set it aside for further investigation and continued to open the rest of the mail, but his mind and his eyes were on that final brown envelope, yet to be opened.

After he had dealt with all the other mail, he turned his attention to the brown envelope which interested him, trying to work out what its contents might be. The postmark was that of 'Oban, Argyllshire.'

He had a dull feeling in the pit of his stomach, what could it be? Good news? *'There's not much good news about these days, apart from the Good News found in the Holy Book,'* he reflected.

*'Was it bad news?'* he wondered, surely not but it seemed that there was nothing *but* bad news on the wireless these days.
As he pondered the possibilities, it struck him that the best way to find out what its contents might be, was to actually open the envelope and put his overactive imagination to rest.

As he came to this decision, the door behind him clicked and a small rather scruffy black cat called Moses entered, announcing his arrival with a loud 'meow.' He jumped up on Colin's knee and curled up, making himself very much at home.
Colin rummaged through the papers on his desk and lifted the paper knife he had received as a gift on his Ordination and slit open the intriguing envelope.

*Dear Sir..."* it began.

*"Item 1 : Subsequent to the passing of your Maternal Grandmother, Mrs Martha McGillivray and in accordance with her Last Will and Testament, I am instructed to inform you that she has bequeathed all her worldly goods, which include the property of the Croft Steading called, 'The Croft' and Land adjacent, situated on the outer-skirts of the village of Kinlochmhor on the Island of Rhua - to you, Colin Shaw Campbell, being her Grandson and sole beneficiary.*

*Item 2 : All this is contingent, as a condition of this legacy, that you, as a Minister of the Church of Scotland, do conduct the funeral service of the said Martha MacGillivary – on Wednesday 27th July 1949 in the Rhua Parish Church, Kinlochmore, The Isle of Rhua.*
*For further details, see attached pages.*
*Your sincerely, etc etc"*

Colin dropped the envelope onto his lap, much to the irritation of Moses. "Well, I never!" he said, "What do you make of that Moses?" to which Moses sneezed, closed his eyes and gave a flick of his tail, perhaps wondering what was so important as to disturb his morning nap.

Colin read the letter through again, checking that it really was *his* name, perhaps there had been some misunderstanding, but no, it was right enough, he was now the proud owner of a Highland Croft, with land, on the Isle of Rhua, wherever that might be!

It was then that he noticed that the date on the Solicitor's communication was the 19th of July and today was the 23rd of July, the letter had taken 4 days to get to him! It was now only 4 days to the date set for the funeral! Oh my!
He hastily copied the Solicitor's contact number onto the back of the envelope and took out his diary.
In what some might consider as 'blind panic' but Colin preferred to think of as 'controlled haste,' he went to the bookshelf for his Ordinance Survey Map of the Highlands and Islands of Scotland to find out exactly where his Highland Estate was.

After much searching, he finally found the small

island of Rhua, like a wee jewel sparkling somewhere West of Coll and North West of Tiree in the Inner Hebrides.

It was more remote than he had envisaged, but then he had hardly ever ventured far from Glasgow, except for weekend climbing trips to Glencoe with his Divinity student pals.

*'Okay,'* he thought to himself, *'I know when and where, the next thing is, how? How on earth am I going to get to Rhua in just 4 days?'*

His first thought was his friend and fellow Divinity student, Iain McDougall who had moved back home to Appin, near Oban, after they had Graduated.

Colin searched through his address book and found Iain's phone number and went out into the hallway to use the communal phone.

In truth, it wasn't so much *Iain's* number, as he didn't have the phone in the house, but rather it was the number for the Appin Post Office where Iain's father was the Postmaster and where Iain helped out most days.

After much crackling and being cut off twice, he finally heard the cheery voice of Iain McDougall, his good friend and ally.

"Oh it's yourself!" bellowed Iain. "How are things in the fleshpots of the 'dear, green place'?" Iain was well over 6 feet 4 inches high with a bushy beard and a deep, booming voice. He was what Colin's mother would have called 'a big strapping lad'.

# Chapter 2

*"Colin was quite sure that his Grandmother had no connections with the Mafia…"*

◆

After catching up with each other's news, Colin was eager to use Iain's local knowledge of the West Coast to plan his journey to Rhua.

"Rhua!?" Iain said, rather too loudly. "My God man, why would anyone want to go away out there!? It's miles from Appin!"

Iain's yardstick as to remoteness was, 'how far is it from Appin?' Appin being the centre of his universe.

As Colin explained the reason for his trip to Rhua, Iain said sympathetically, "Oh dear, may God rest your dear grandmother's soul. My condolence to you and your family, Colin."

He said that it *was* possible to make it in time for the funeral – but it would be tight.

Colin would have to take a bus up to Oban first thing in the morning, then a boat out to Coll and take a further boat over to Rhua. It could well turn out to be a 2 or 3 day trip, assuming the good Lord was with him and Colin had no doubt that He would be.

"I have a cousin, Donald John on Coll who has a fine looking boat." Iain said in his beautiful highland lilt. "If you can get yourself to Coll as soon as the wind will carry you, he will take you over to Rhua in time for the funeral - he'll make sure of that."

"Thank you so much Iain," Colin said warmly, "Perhaps we might meet up in Oban on my way back?"

"That would be grand," replied Iain "and maybe we can take a 'wee glass' for old times' sake."

Colin had some traumatic memories of 'taking a wee glass to be sociable' with Iain, and his liver was still in the recovery stage from the last time they met.

"That would be great," Colin said with little enthusiasm, "Please tell your mother that I am asking kindly for her," and hung up.

At some point during their climbing trips to Glencoe, they invariably took the MacBraynes bus for the 17 mile trip from Glencoe down to Appin to visit Iain's mother.

She would give them a hearty meal and dry out their clothes, apply Calamine Lotion on the many midgie bites they would have received, and give them a nice soft bed for the night.

Happy days indeed – but why was so much of it a blur?

Perhaps it was the size of the drams she would pour for them. The good Lord would understand and it was well known that the size of the drams were just a measure of Mrs McDougall's kind hospitality and it would be most unkind to refuse.

*"Oh dear, Highland thinking,"* Colin said to himself. He had spent too much time with Iain MacDougall!

*'So, that's sorted,'* he thought, *'what next?'*
*'You mean, apart from contacting the Solicitor in Oban, putting together the Service for his grandmother, packing and getting over to Rhua in time?'*

He felt his blood pressure rise at the thought of it all.

"Okay Colin, you'll need to calm down," he said out loud as he walked through to the kitchenette, followed by his faithful wee pal Moses.

With a cup of tea and a custard cream biscuit in hand, he made his way back through to his study, with Moses at his heels.

He tore a page out of his notebook and being an extremely organized person, almost to the point of being obsessively so, he laid out his thoughts in order by listing all that he had to do.

Number 1 – Phone the Solicitor in Oban to -
     (a) confirm the details
     (b) obtain more information
Number 2 – Organize travel arrangements
Number 3 – Borrow suitcase from Aunty
            Bunty in Bearsden
Number 4 – Draft out an Order of Service for the Funeral service.

*'Anything else?'* he thought to himself.

As his mind began to wander, thoughts of his grandmother came into his head.

What did he *really* know about the late Martha McGillivray? *'Not a lot'* ran through his mind, apart from the time that she and his grandfather had visited Glasgow from the Islands a number of years ago.

They spoke a very different language to your average 'Glasgow Keelie' he remembered. He had managed to pick out the occasional word or two but there seemed to be another tongue in there somewhere.
Of course, now, he realised that it was the Gaelic, still so prevalent in the Islands and Highlands even now.

He remembered that his mother had occasionally used Gaelic words, but when he had pushed her to use it more – she simply said, "Wheeesht!, it's not a tongue for the well bred to be speaking!" and would swiftly change the subject.
His Mother's attitude towards her native tongue had always led him to believe that it was something to be ashamed of, or at least not something to be proud of. Whereas his pal Iain and a few other Divinity pals from the Islands seemed to be inordinately proud of their ancient language. The fact that they would often meet in

huddles in the Student's Rec. room and talk in their strange tongue, had earned them the by-name of the 'Gaelic Mafia,' by the other students.

He was quite sure that his grandmother had no connections with the Mafia. The very thought of her in her pinny and rollers being a 'gangster's moll' made him laugh out loud, before pulling himself up, abruptly thinking, *'Ok, let's get serious!'*

He picked up the telephone and asked the operator to put him through to the Oban number for Messrs MacDonald, MacDonald and MacDonald, Solicitors and Notary.

After much crackling, Colin heard a faint voice saying, "Hello! Hello! Is it yourself that is calling?"

"Yes, it is me," Colin found himself saying, to which came the reply.

"Now don't you be worrying, I'm going to get you off all of the charges! She can't prove a thing, we'll take her for every penny. I can find witnesses to show you weren't even there at the time." Colin found it necessary to interrupt and protest his innocence. "Stop! This is absurd, I am the Rev Colin Campbell and I am calling about the funeral service for the late Mrs Martha McGillivray!" he said in his most sombre Ministerial voice, a tone which he only employed for Prayers and Funerals.

The line went silent for a moment but Colin knew there was still someone there, he could tell by the breathing and a stressed voice saying, "O God! O God!" in a panic stricken voice.
"No, it is not God," said Colin "but a man of the cloth nevertheless! Now, what on earth is going on!?" The poor man in Oban was so flustered all he could say was, "I'm sorry. I must have got the wrong number!" and immediately hung up.

Colin stood in his study holding the telephone, wondering what on earth had just happened as Moses wrapped himself around the telephone cord playfully.
He immediately redialled and the voice at the other end was unmistakably the same man he had

just spoken to. "Was it yourself I was just speaking to?" Colin said in his best Highland voice – *his grandmother would have been proud.*

"Er.. no, it was another number you must have connected to, how can I help?" said the Solicitor having calmed himself. Colin smiled.

The arrangements were made and helpfully the Oban Solicitor added, *'In the case of any emergency such as the boat capsizing in the rough seas and all hands lost, then the Free Church Minister, Rev Farquhar McCrimmond, is ready and waiting to take the service'.*

"Oh good," Colin had said weakly but was not sure what exactly was 'good' about it.

Things were beginning to take shape.

Items 1 and 2 on the list could now be struck off his 'to do' list.

Item 3 – 'borrow the family suitcase from Aunty Bunty in Bearsden', was next to be addressed.

Time was of the essence if he was to leave first thing in the morning, so there was nothing else for it but to go up there and pick it up himself.

After putting Moses into the kitchenette and pouring a saucer of milk, he donned his helmet, put on his leather jacket and gloves and went round to the garden shed.

He rolled out his pride and joy, a 1938 BSA Goldstar 500 cc. motorbike - and after a few kicks of the kick-start, the engine burst into life and away he flew, juking between the jaywalkers and the slow moving trams, up through Maryhill, past the lovely Abbotsford House, over to Bearsden Cross and round the corner to his Aunty Bunty's.

# Chapter 3

*"Aye, feet certainly run in the family…"*

◆

Aunty Bunty was a cheery soul, always ready with a smile and a scone whatever time of day or night anyone might arrive at her door.

Colin had a special place in his heart for his Aunty Bunty who had been a great support to him after his mother passed on just a few years ago.

"You'll stay for a wee cup of tea and a scone Colin." It was more of a statement of fact than a question. "I can't stay Aunty, I'm away up to the Highlands in the morning and I have a hundred and one things to do yet, so if I could just pick up the suitcase, I'll be on my way," Colin replied.

"Would you like a cup of tea and a wee scone?" Aunty Bunty repeated, absent mindedly. "Take a seat in the front room and I'll bring it through to you, you being a Minster and all," she said with more than a hint of pride in her voice.

As Aunty Bunty busied herself in the kitchen,

Colin looked around the front room. It was dated even for his conservative taste. The three-piece suite had been there since he had played on it as a child many years ago. The net curtains had seen better days, as had the linoleum, on top of which was an 'Axminster rug' in front of the fireplace, at least 'Axminster' was what his Aunt Bunty called it.

Whenever the children had lemonade or cakes, she would say loudly, "Mind the Axminster children!" so that any visitors could hear quite clearly.

Colin's mind took him back to his childhood, playing on that very same 'Axminster' – but somewhere in the dark recesses of his mind, he seemed to remember being told that his Uncle Bill, Aunty Bunty's late husband, brought it home from the Barras' market.

His Aunt appeared with a tray laden with scones, rock cakes and pancakes – enough to feed the whole of the H.L.I. (*Highland Light Infantry - a local Glasgow Regiment*).

"Now eat up," she urged Colin, "this will keep you going until you get up to Hyndland."

Colin nearly choked on his scone and said, "I'm going up to the Highlands Aunty Bunty, the *Highlands,* not Hyndland!" to which Aunty Bunty replied, "Oh dear me! Whatever are you going away up there for? Is it thon Lassie from Aberdeen that you met in that University you'll be going to see? You're too young for the Lassies!"

"Oh mercy, no Aunty – you'll not have heard, Granny Martha has passed on," Colin explained solemnly.

"Oh glory be! God rest her soul. It will be a blessed release, she had an awful time with her feet for years, if it wasn't one foot it was the other." Aunty Bunty said solemnly.

"Your poor mother, God bless her, didn't have her troubles to seek, just like myself. She was always under the Doctor with her feet.

"Aye, feet have always run in the family."

Colin nearly choked for the second time, this time on a particularly hard lump of rock cake as he waited for Aunty Bunty to smile, but her remarks had flown completely over her own head.

Seizing the moment, Colin stood up and said firmly, "Oh well Aunty, I'd better be making a move – lots to do and so little time!"

"Aye, 'just as it is in life,' that's what our Minister, the Reverend McMaster says.

Oh, wait you, I nearly forgot to give you the suitcase, that would never do," and she went through to the bedroom and came back with a medium sized, brown suitcase which had 'W. Campbell RN' and his Service number stencilled on the top. It has certainly seen better days.

"That saw your uncle Billy right through the war, thick and thin. It's just as well that he didn't get any further than Portsmouth before he was sent home with his legs, or we wouldn't have that case in the family today."

"Gosh, Aunty. Is that right?" was all Colin could find to say in response.

He picked up the shabby case, kissed Aunty Bunty on the cheek and made for the door, sensing freedom was only a few paces away.

Just as he opened the front door, Aunty Bunty called from the Kitchen. "Wait now, here is a bag of scones for your journey!"

Once outside, he wasted no time in getting the small case tied onto the panniers of the motorbike, with the scones safely stowed inside.
He donned his helmet and gloves and with a wave, sped off down to Bearsden Cross and then home.
Aunty Bunty said a short prayer as Colin roared away.

That was item 3 ticked off his 'to do' list.
And now for Item 4, 'Draft out an Order of Service for the Funeral.'

Having stroked Moses and given him a few biscuits, Colin made himself a cup of tea, took two custard creams and went through to this study and sat in quiet contemplation.
*'What can I say about someone I hardly knew?'* he thought to himself.
He sat for a while in thoughtful silence, then he picked up a pencil and wrote, *"You all knew*

*Martha so well, so what can I say that you don't already know… so let us bring our thoughts of our dearly departed Martha to our Creator God, let us bow our heads in prayer."*

Now he was on more familiar ground. Praying was what he was good at and so he wrote a few lines as a prompt, knowing that he would extemporise on the day.

When looking for the right words, the Holy Spirit had always given them to him. He knew that once he had spoken the first few words, *"We are gathered here as sinners in the sight of the Lord…"* in his best 'Ministerial' voice, he would be up and running, so to speak.

After another few rushes of Divine inspiration, Colin was satisfied with his rough outline of the Funeral Service and put his notes and his King James Bible into Uncle Bill's suitcase.

Pyjamas and a few other necessary items were packed, ready for the 'journey into the unknown,' in the morning.

He made a few phone calls and before long Bus

and McBrayne's boat times were jotted into his notebook.

Time for a bit of supper and a good night's sleep, the next few days were going to be tiring and it was all going to be starting, very early tomorrow morning.
Moses was fed and put out for the night. It had been a long day, time for bed.

# Chapter 4

*"Gonnie bless my bottle o' Holy wine Father?..."*

◆

Colin's small travel alarm clock began to buzz annoyingly at 5 am.

*'Surely it isn't time to get up already!?'* Colin mumbled to himself. It seemed no time since he had said his prayers, slipped between the sheets and turned off the bedside lamp.

The bus for Oban was leaving at 6.30 am so there was no time to 'dilly dally' as his Aunty Bunty would say.

Colin rose, made up his bed and got himself ready for his long journey up to the Inner Hebrides.

He fed Moses, adding an extra spoonful, perhaps to assuage his guilt for leaving him.

"Oh well, Moses my trusty friend, I'll not be seeing you for a few days but Mrs McRae will be in as usual and will make sure you're fed and cared for in my absence. Be sure and behave now."

Suddenly Colin felt quite emotional - as the

importance and the immensity of the next few days suddenly struck him.

Was he *really* going to a remote Island, to a place he had never been and knew nothing about, to conduct a funeral service for a grandmother he had only met once or twice?

A fleeting thought ran in, and then out, of his mind. Perhaps he could phone and arrange for the Free Church Minister on Rhua to take the service on some pretext or another? The thought didn't linger in his head for more than a few seconds. No, of course he couldn't do that, it would be disrespectful to the memory of his dear, late grandmother.

He left the bag of Aunty Bunty's scones on the kitchen table with a note saying, *"Dear Mrs McRae, I have had to go away for a few days, not sure how long I will be, would you please look after Moses in my absence. Here are a few of my Aunty Bunty's scones to take home with you.*

*Many thanks.*
*Regards. Colin."*

She would see them in the morning when she came into clean.

Colin put on his outer coat, closed his eyes and said a prayer for a safe journey, then stepped out of the house and made his way down to the Kelvinhall underground station. As usual, it was raining.

He got off at Enoch Square and just a short walk across Argyll Street and up West Nile Street took him up to the Dundas Street Bus station.

Colin was surprised to see how busy Glasgow was at that time of the morning. Some people were just starting their day as others were making their weary way home.

It had been over a year since his Ordination, and Colin was still feeling conspicuous when wearing his Clerical Collar, and he was getting quite a few glances from passers by. *'Maybe they are wondering what I am doing up so early,'* he mused. *'Perhaps they think I'm on a mission of mercy to some poor soul.'* But his thoughts were rudely interrupted by a deep, hoarse voice shouting, "Gonnie gie's a few bob Father?"

It was a wee dishevelled man, worse the wear for a bottle (or two) of cheap, fortified wine. The man shouted again, "Hey Father! Gonnie bless my bottle o' Holy wine?" followed by a raucous laugh as he saw the embarrassment on the young Minister's face.

Colin quickened his pace as he went into the Bus station and looked for the Bluebird bus for Oban. He asked a group of drivers and conductresses who were catching up with their latest news, to which one answered, "This is it here Father, jump on or ye'll be too late!"

Colin looked up at the destination displayed on the front of the bus and saw that it said, Tyndrum. "But...but..." he protested.

"Gonnie get oan!?" a conductress said firmly, taking his small case and placing it in the compartment under the bus.

Colin thought it best not to argue, so he climbed on and slipped into a seat, keeping his coat collar up and his hat down until the bus pulled away.

Just as it was leaving Parliament Street, the clippie came and asked him, "Where to, Father?" Colin wished people would stop calling him 'Father.'

"I'm going to Oban," he replied.

"No' on this bus ye're no' she said."

"What! You mean I am on the wrong bus!?" Colin stood up. "Calm down Father," (there it was again). I'm just pulling your leg, you'll have to change on to the MacBraynes Highland bus at Tyndrum to get the rest of the way to Oban."

She smiled and winked at Colin who immediately turned a bright red, redder than Satan's Sunday suit.

He looked out of the window, the rain was getting heavier. 'Typical Glasgow weather,' he thought as the bus juddered its weary way North.

Colin was feeling quite low and very much out of his comfort zone, so he took out the small Bible which he kept in his coat pocket and read from the Book of Daniel at Chapter 6, 'Daniel in the Lion's Den,' for comfort.

The bus passed through Alexandria, stopping in Luss to pick up two hikers, and then on up Loch Lomond side. Colin became drowsy and his mind darted from one thing to another.

He thought of Carole, "Carol with an E!" as she used to say. The girl he had met in Uni, the girl from a wee place called Keith, in Banffshire, that his Aunty had talked about. Colin remembered her long red hair, her smile and her sharp intellectual mind.

He smiled to himself when he remembered how, with her strong Doric accent, she would call his Aunty Bunty, 'Unty Bunty' and they would both laugh.

He always felt guilty for laughing at his lovely Aunt, but Carole said it was just harmless fun. He wondered if he would ever see her again.

They had parted on that last day at Glasgow University with a, "Keep in touch," and the reply, "You too," as they went their separate ways.

Then he remembered that he didn't have her home address in Keith, and his heart sank at the thought perhaps that meeting in the Students Rec. Room in the University may well have been their last, he hoped not.

He sighed and looked out of the window, it was still raining, indeed, if anything, it was getting worse. The mist was now coming down like a soft grey blanket falling over the hillside.

Even the sheep looked fed up.

His eyes closed and he dozed off into a deep sleep. Suddenly, a sharp jolt shook the bus with a loud "Get out of the way ye daft buggers!" from the driver. Colin sat bolt upright, what on earth was going on?

The driver glanced into his interior mirror and saw Colin looking down the aisle of the bus, and on seeing the dog collar he shouted, "Sorry Father! It's the bloody deer on the road!"

"Oh, sorry Father!" his face went bright red when he realised that he had just uttered a second oath, and to a Minister too!

There were a few chuckles from the passengers who had seen what was going on, Colin blushed and sat down. Picking up his Bible he turned to the Gospel of Matthew Chapter 17 at verse 2, *"and he was transfigured before them and his face shone like the sun..."*

The journey along the side of Loch Lomond was a bumpy, twisty one, interspersed with curses from the driver as he berated the sheep and occasional deer for having the cheek to be crossing the road just as he was wanting by.

Soon, sleep overcame him, and he nodded off once more, this time into a deeper sleep.
Strange fantasies flew around his mind, bizarre imaginings, irrational and absurd in nature.
A large seal appeared in his dream which smiled at him before morphing into a beautiful mermaid.
Then he saw a large stag with a fierce look on his face, fairies dancing in a ring to the most beautiful music, and otters chasing a horse into the sea.
Suddenly the music stopped.
Silence.

The strange images turned and stared at him and a chill ran down his spine.
Was it just a bad dream or something more sinister like a premonition of things to come?
Whatever it was, it unnerved Colin.

Suddenly he was wakened by the conductress shouting, "All change for Lochawe, Taynuilt and Oban. Father, that means you!"

# Chapter 5

*"A young man like yourself had better be watching
out, the Coll lassies like the young men,
especially when they're Meenisters..."*

•

He looked out of the window, still shaking from
his unnerving dream and saw a signpost that
indicated they had stopped at, 'Tyndrum Lower.'
He quickly stirred himself, grabbed his hat and
coat and scurried down to the front of the bus, still
half asleep.

The conductress stood waiting to hand Colin his
case.

"That's yer bus ower there," she pointed to a pale
green and red MacBraynes bus. "Take care of
yourself Father and don't let those highland
lassies be taking advantage of such a young man
as yourself!" she said with a smile and a wink.

Colin blushed and handed his case to the
MacBraynes driver who placed it in the locker
under the bus and looked at his watch, indicating
that Colin should hurry up.

At least the rain was beginning to ease off.

"The Lord waits for no man Father," he said with a glower.

"Is it not, '*Time* waits for no man'?" Colin thought as he quickened his step - and along with the two hikers they had picked up at Luss, boarded the MacBraynes bus.

Colin made his way down the bus and settled himself into a seat.

'*Not long now,*' he thought, not really knowing how long it would be before arriving in Oban but after such an already long journey he felt it surely couldn't be much further now.

He closed his eyes and before he knew it, he was fast asleep once more.

Memories, Bible readings and prayerful words flowed into his mind which were so vivid that they woke him up with a start.

He felt sure they were coming from his faithful God. He took out his notebook but hardly had time to write them down before another word or phrase came into his mind.

This 'divine conversation' was interrupted by the conductress saying in a lovely soft highland lilt, "May I be seeing your ticket, Father?"

Colin was caught completely off guard. His mind was on a 'higher plane' and panic began to set in as he couldn't remember getting a ticket!

"I... I'm sorry..." he stuttered as he rummaged through his pockets. "I don't remember getting one," he said with great embarrassment.

"A likely story Father," said the conductress with a smile. "You Meenisters are always trying it on with us lassies."

"No, no, honestly, I didn't mean to... I wouldn't do such a thing..." Colin stumbled over his words as he searched his pockets, his face now a bright shade of scarlet.

"Where are you going to, Meenister?" the conductress asked.

"Rhua, but I'm stopping over at Coll for the night," Colin answered as he continued to look for his ticket.

"Oh, a young man like yourself had better be watching out, the Coll lassies like the young men, especially when they're Meenisters," the conductress turned away to hide a smile.

"Oh dear... oh dear... I'm... er..." Between having no ticket and hearing about the young ladies on Coll, he was all a fluster.

"Och, don't you be worrying Father, it was just a joke I was having. We don't take money from men of the cloth as they go about the good Lord's business, besides, we never know the day we might be needing them." She gave him a smile and moved on down the bus collecting tickets and fares from those who had joined the bus at Tyndrum and Loch Awe, occasionally looking back at him and giving a coy smile.

It seemed no time before they were pulling into Oban bus station where all were reunited with their luggage.

"Take care Father," said the conductress with a smile and a wink, "And watch out for those Call girls!" she added.

Colin's hat nearly fell off at the mention of 'Call Girls.' The conductress laughed out loudly saying, "The girls from Coll!" she clarified. "Watch out for them – they have a liking for men of the cloth!"

Colin's face flushed as he hurried off down to Oban pier, shaking his head at the very thought of call girls on Coll, whatever next.

A scruffy, surly looking Porter with a grubby sailor's cap, was leaning against a wall finishing off the last puff of his cigarette as Colin passed by. The Porter tipped his cap towards the young Minister, thinking to himself, *'Mercy me, it's younger these Meenisters are getting!'* But he smartened up as Colin stopped and looked at him. The Porter was unnerved - *'Mercy me,'* he thought, *'has he the second sight and is hearing my thinking?'*

"Would you be so kind as to tell me which is the boat to Coll?" Colin asked.

The Porter dropped the remains of his cigarette, stubbed it out with his foot, and said, "Oh aye Meenister, that will be her over there at the South Pier, 'The Lochearn'," nodding towards a large boat with two high masts (*for it is bad luck to point at boats*) adding, by way of noteworthy information, "Aye, she has just had two new fancy engines fitted, she's as fine a boat as ever sailed the Sound of Mull."

Colin struggled to understand all that the Porter had said, it was a mix of broken English and the Gaelic, it reminded him of his grandmother, Martha.

"Thank you," Colin politely replied. The Porter gave Colin a slight bow as he sauntered off.

Then he turned and said, "Oh, and be sure to get on with the right foot, or your journey will be troubled," in an ominous tone. What could he mean?

The strange sideways glance and the peculiar remark unnerved Colin. Was it awkwardness at being in the company of a man of the cloth? Perhaps, but Colin sensed something else, was it a warning of trouble ahead?

Colin made his way over to the South Pier and began to board the Lochearn. The porter was right, it was a fine looking ship.

As he walked across the narrow wooden gangway, he took a wee slip and grabbed the rope which was a makeshift handrail. "Be careful Meenister, we wouldn't want you to be having any accidents while you're aboard!" a voice shouted.

Colin looked up and saw a group of Sailors with their loose serge trousers, pea jackets and black caps, watching him. Colin smiled nonchalantly and scurried across and onto the boat. He heard the crew speaking in the Gaelic and then a great laugh got up and he somehow knew that he was the butt of a joke.

A ruddy looking crew member with a white beard and smoking a short, stubby pipe met Colin as he boarded the boat. "Welcome aboard the Lochearn, as fine a boat as ever sailed the Sound of Mull!" he said with pride. "My name is Donald MacRae, first Mate," and before Colin could respond, the old sailor continued, "Is it yourself that will be taking poor Martha McGillivray's funeerial service, Meenister?"

"Yes," said Colin, "but how did you know?"

"My cousin Hector's wife is from Rhua and it was herself that told me," the old sea dog answered. "Aye she told me that a Meenister would be coming up from Glaschu, but never did I think he would be just out of the school!"

"Oh well," Colin replied, "maturity isn't dependent on age."

"Aye, just that!" the old mariner said as he spat out a stream of black bogey-roll tobacco juice over the side, wondering what on earth Colin was talking about.

"You'll er... I mean um.... You'll not be walking around the boat will you Meenister?" Donald McRae seemed agitated and stuttered awkwardly. "You can sit in the lounge for the duration. It'll keep you safe, you know, just in case of, well, um, accidental incidents and such like."

Colin saw that look again, the same look as he had seen from the Porter on the pier. A look that smacked of unease and fear.

"But why on earth would I want to sit in the lounge for the whole of the voyage, it's about 4 or 5 hours or so, isn't it?"

"Well, it's….. it's…. a superstition among us seafaring folk, it's… it's bad luck to have 'men of the cloth' onboard."

"But what harm could *I* possibly bring to your boat?"

The old sailor looked around and said in a whisper, "It is said that 'Black Donald' (*ie Donald dhu, the devil*) himself is never far away when Meenisters are around, bringing misadventure and cata-strophies and such like."

"Don't worry Mr McRae, I promise to behave myself."

"Aye, well…" said the First Mate, still convinced that they were all doomed.

He gave Colin a black look and ambled off.

Some of the crew followed on, talking among themselves in the Gaelic and looking back at Colin, trying not to catch his eye.

*'Never look the devil in the eye,'* as the old saying goes,'

# Chapter 6

*"Strange things can happen to*
*Meenisters out here..."*

◆

The whole encounter with the old sailor had left young Colin quite shaken although he tried not to show it.

*'I'll never get used to the ways of the Highlands,'* he thought to himself as he walked through a doorway and found himself in a small lounge area where he was grateful to see some soft seating.

He looked around at the handful of passengers, some were tourists and others were probably locals making their way home.

Colin found a corner seat and made himself comfortable.

"What will you be having, Meenister?" a voice from above said to Colin. He looked up to see a dark haired Steward standing over him. "Could I have a small sherry please?"

"Yes, you could Meenister, if we had any," the Steward said with a smile. "Our complete range is Whisky or bottled beer, which would you prefer?

Oh, and we also have bottles of Lager, but that's just for the ladies, of course."

"Oh dear," said Colin, not knowing what to do, he wasn't a drinker, not like his good friend Iain in Appin who was known to take a fair dram.

The Steward saw Colin's dilemma and bent down and whispered in his ear, "I quite understand Meenister, it wouldn't be seemly for you to be seen with a glass of whisky and a bottle of beer as a chaser. How about if I pour a bottle of McEwans Export into a mug, and no-one will be any the wiser!?"
The day had been long and tiring, and perhaps the Steward's idea wasn't such a bad one in the circumstances. Colin nodded to the Steward. The good Lord would understand.

This was the first sea voyage that Colin had ever undertaken and he felt very apprehensive, but then he remembered a text in the book of Psalms and took out his Bible and turned to Psalm 95.
He scanned 'the word' until he found what he was looking for, at verse 3, "*The Lord is the great God,*

*the great King of all gods. In His hands are the depths of the earth, the mountain peaks belong to Him. The sea is His, for it was He who made it…"*

The words gave him great comfort and he knew that the great God of the Universe was right there with him as he set out on his journey to Coll and onward to the tiny island of Rhua. Even if Colin didn't know where Rhua was, he was quite sure that God did!

A few minutes later the Steward returned with a tea towel over his arm. He carried a tray on which was a large mug with the 'Camp Coffee' logo on the side. He placed it on the small table in front of Colin and said in an exaggerated actorial voice, "Your ..er.. *'Coffee'* Meenister," with a wink.

Colin surveyed the few people sitting around but no-one seemed to notice, except perhaps the two Muileachs (*Moolachs, natives of Mull*) who looked at each other and smiled.
They'd seen it all before.

He settled down with a mug of 'coffee' in one hand and his Bible in the other.

Closing his eyes he took a deep breath and exhaled slowly three times. Feeling calmer he took out his notepad and set about putting the final touches to his grandmother's "funeerial" service, as Donald McRae, the old sailor, had called it.

He spent quite a while making sense of the many scribbled notes, words and passages that had been 'given' to him while sleeping on the bus.

Colin smiled to himself as he recognized that it was the Holy Spirit who had given him the words he needed to say, and he felt quite dizzy with excitement at the thought of it - or was it the McEwan's Export that had fired him up?

He was working on these, 'divinely inspired' words for the funeral, when he felt the boat list to one side as it turned in towards a Pier with a row of houses alongside, all painted different bright colours.
As he looked out of the porthole, he saw red, blue and yellow houses. "Is this Coll?" he said to whoever was listening.

"No Meenister, this would be Tobermory," one of the Muileachs answered as they made their way down to the lower deck, ready to step onto the beautiful Island of Mull and make their way home.

Colin felt the need for some fresh air, so he made his way up on deck where he saw passengers disembarking down the short gangway. Some were met by family and others walked up to the two Bowman's buses which were waiting to take them on to other parts of Mull. One bus indicated it was going to 'BUNESSAN for IONA' and the other showed that it was going across to 'DERVAIG' where there were plans for a Bear Park to be created, which brought about the by-name of a 'Bear' to be attributed to someone from that historic village.

Parcels, boxes and large packages were offloaded onto the jetty and before long he saw a young boy untie the end of the rope from the capstan and throw it into the water as the engines rumbled and the boat slowly made its way out of Tobermory Bay.

"Next stop, Coll," Donald MacRae said to Colin who jumped as he hadn't seen the old sailor standing beside him.

"Should you not be going back inside Meenister? You might catch some tropical disease or some such thing," said Duncan. "You'll not be wanting that, now, would you?"

"Tropical disease – in Scotland?" Colin replied. "Surely not."

"Aye, well," Donald said with a sinister look. "You never know, strange things can happen to Meenisters out here…" he said in an sinister voice. "It might be better if you was to go back inside and maybe have another cup of *'coffee'*," he said with a wink.

Did he know about the 'coffee' ruse? Colin wondered, or perhaps a midgie had got into Donald's eye. Either way, he thought it best to go back inside – and just what did the old timer mean by, *"Strange things can happen to Meenisters out here?"*

Colin closed his eyes and gave up a prayer, asking for the good Lord's protection in this strange place full of strange people with their ancient tongue and mysterious ways.

He felt much better after the prayer and made his way back down to his table in the lounge where his Bible and notepad were waiting for him.
"Another '*coffee*', Meenister?" the Steward smiled.
"Better not, thank you," Colin answered, "better keep a clear head."
"Aye, just as you say," agreed the Steward as Colin sat down.

As he looked around, feeling rather lost and alone in an alien environment, his mind wandered to his University friend, Carole (with an E) and he wished she were here with him now. She was always good company and a steady hand in difficult times. He could do with her positive, 'all will be well' attitude just now.
Had he made a mistake in not getting in touch with her since they left University? Well, she could just as easily have got in touch with him, but '*no*' he thought, it was *his* place to contact her, him being the man.

He decided he would get in touch with her once he was home from the funeral, if he ever made it back to civilization, that was!

Alternating between reading, taking notes and dozing, the sea journey passed quite quickly. So much so that when he heard the Tannoy System announce, *"Listen you here - make ready for those who are going to be disembarking at Coll as we are going to be arriving there in just a wee while."* Colin was quite taken aback and hurriedly put his Bible and notepad into his case and stood up ready for the next leg of his, 'journey into the unknown.'

He was surprised that no-one else seemed to be stirring themselves, perhaps he was the only one getting off at Coll.

"Now don't you be harassing yourself Meenister," a voice behind him said. "The Captain likes to give the tourists a wee bit warning in case they should be taking a dram, so they don't have to rush the experience."

Colin looked round to see Donald MacRae smiling a toothless smile.

"It's not like the train to Ballachulish where you jump off and keep running, just before it stops. We'll be a wee while yet Meenister, I'll come back for you incase you miss your destination!"

Sure enough, about 20 minutes or so later, the old seafarer called on Colin, "It's time that we are nearly there Meenister!" and Colin rose and followed his new found friend down to the boat deck.

"Watch out for the Call girls Meenister!" a voice shouted out followed by much cheering and laughing from a group of the crew.
Colin nonchalantly replied, "Oh, *that* old joke!?" as if he had heard it many times before, and smiled as he felt he had got one over on the old sea dogs.

As the Lochearn came alongside, a rope was thrown over to a waiting young lad who caught it and pulled it up until he got to the larger rope which he tied in a figure of eight between 2 rusty bollards.

The wooden gangway was laid across to the jetty and the passengers walked shakily across.

Colin waved at Donald MacRae, turned, and walked along the jetty to a boathouse where a young woman stood waiting.

# Chapter 7

*"…there's no' a fish that's safe when
Callum McLeod is around…"*

◆

"Is it yourself, Meenister?" the young woman asked. "Yes, the collar kind of gives it away, don't you think?" Colin replied and shook her hand saying, "And you are….?"

"Oh, yes, I'm Rhona, Donald John's wife. I have to take you up to the Croft for something to eat and a dram," Rhona replied as she picked up Colin's suitcase and took off up the road at a fair pace, leaving Colin to catch up.

Rhona left the road and walked along the shoreline path with Colin behind, trying to catch up.

After about half a mile, she stopped at the gate of a small croft and turned round to see a red faced Colin as he puffed his way along behind her.

"Och man," Rhona smiled as she spoke, "You city folk are not used to the walking! Come away in, himself will be glad to meet you, he has a new bottle of the whisky that wants to try and he'd like your opinion. *'One thing about Meenisters,'* he always says, is *'they know a good dram when they taste one.'*

Rhona entered the croft and seeing no sign of her husband she shouted, "Donald John, where are you?"
A voice came from the back of the croft but Colin couldn't make out what he was saying as he was speaking to Rhona in the Gaelic, their native tongue.
Rhona turned to Colin saying, "He's out the back stacking the peats, he'll be in just shortly. I'll show you to your room and you can leave your case and your coat there for now. I'll put another peat on the fire and we'll have a wee strupag (*cup of tea*) when you come through."

Colin left his bits and pieces on the bed and went back through to join Rhona.
He had just sat down when Donald John came into the house. He was a tall, broad shouldered man with a swarthy appearance and a big smile. "Hello Meeenister, Ciamera a tha thu an-diugh? (*Cimmera ha an joo. How are you today?*).

62

Colin's good friend Iain McDougal, had taught him that the reply to this greeting was "*Tha mi gle mhath!* (*Ha me gley vaa. I am very well*) so Colin responded accordingly.

Donald John's smile broadened and he laughed saying, "Well done! I see you are learning to speak in God's own tongue!" and he invited Colin to sit down.

"So, is it Rhua that you are going to?" he asked Colin, although he already knew the answer. "Yes, it's for my grandmother's funeral, God rest her soul." Donald John already knew that too, but it is customary to make polite conversation when first meeting someone.

"Aye, she was a lovely lady," Donald John said with a wistful air. "She was a martyr to her legs." "So I believe," Colin answered, wondering if that had any relevance to anything. Perhaps he should mention her legs in the funeral service? Perhaps not.

"I'm looking forward to seeing my grandparents' croft, will I be able to stay there for the next few days?" Colin asked.

"Well, I thought it best if you stayed with someone, seeing as you are on your own, so I have arranged for you to take lodgings with Mrs McLeod for a couple of nights. She is my mother's half-sister and runs a B & B on Rhua.

Her husband Callum is a rogue. He's an awful man for the Poaching, known all over the Western Isles for it. Man, there's no' a fish that's safe when Callum McLeod is around – but he is a topper of a lad besides that.

Mrs McLeod's grandfather was the Free Church Meenister but he had to give that up when he passed away." Donald John shook his head.

"What a shame," Colin said, not being sure if Donald John was being humorous, but on reflection he thought that passing away wasn't a suitable topic for amusement.

In a complete change of mood, Donald John said, "I am thinking I'll take you over to Rhua in the morning, the funeral is arranged for 3 o'clock, then there will be the wake in the evening in the village hall and you'll not feel like travelling on the next day, so how about if I come for you on the day after that, Friday. You can spend a day or two with us on Coll and then we can see about getting you over to Oban, how does all that sound?

"Well, yes, that all sounds good to me, although I'm not sure if I'll stay for the wake."

A crashing sound came from the kitchen as a cup fell and smashed onto the stone floor. Rhona came through and said, "Oh, you *have* to stay to the wake, Mr McCrimmond, the Free Church Minister would never dream of missing a wake, he says it's the best part of a funeral. He takes a fair dram through the week, and then preaches the evils of the demon drink on the Sabbath!

You can't be letting the Church of Scotland side down Meenister, they will all be looking for you to show a good example and match him dram for dram!"

For the second time in just a few minutes, Colin found himself lost for words, and then he stirred himself to say, "I…I…don't know about that.

I usually only take orange juice or perhaps a sweet sherry when out in company."

Rhona and Donald John looked at each other with a look which was a blend of, *'I don't believe what I am hearing'* and *'Is he joking?'*

There was an awkward silence for a few moments broken by a loud laugh as Donald John said, "Ha ha, you are good at the jokes Meenister! You had us going there for a minute or two… orange juice or a 'sweet sherry' indeed!"

Colin smiled weakly, "Yes, a joke, of course…"

"Aye, it's a character that you are!" Donald John said slapping Colin boisterously on the back.

"Rhona, will you bring that bottle of Jura through? The Meenister is wondering what it tastes like," he winked at Colin.

That was news to him but thought it best not to intervene between husband and wife. "Oh, and two glasses, I might have wee taste myself, just to be sociable, and besides, it wouldn't be polite to see the Meenister drinking on his own."

Rhona came through with the bottle of whisky and two glasses, "You old rogue!" she laughed. "It is yourself that's leading the Meenister astray!" She gave Colin a smile and said, "Never mind Donald John, it's the devil himself that's in him!"

"Oh dear!" Colin was wondering if an exorcism was going to be needed.
On seeing Colin's serious expression, Rhona laughed and explained that it was just a turn of phrase.
"Thank goodness for that!" Colin said and reached over for the glass of 'amber bead' that Donald John was offering him.

In one swift movement, Rhona took a small glass out of the pocket in her apron, filled it with whisky, said, "*Slanj*!" knocked it back, put the glass back into the pocket and disappeared back into the kitchen.
Colin was lost for words and it was Donald John who broke the silence by saying, "Aye, she has the good taste in whisky, Meenister, a great qualification for a wife!"

Donald John poured out two good sized drams handed one to Colin and said, "Well Meenister, bottoms up!.... Oh, er, sorry, I mean, slanj!"

Colin wondered how he was going to get out of drinking the glass of whisky, without giving the game away that he was no drinker.

# Chapter 8

*"The Coll girls…"*

◆

As if on cue, the front door opened and, two young girls appeared, they were Donald John and Rhona's teenage daughters.

"Hello!" they said in unison, "It's only us, the Coll girls!" followed by a fit of laughter.

"Oh mercy, come away in you two!" Rhona said. "These are our daughters, Mhàiri and Kirsty, and girls, this is the Meenister I told you about."
They looked at the young Minister and giggled shyly. "Oh mum!" Mhàiri said, "you didn't say he was going to be so good looking!" and they giggled even more.
"Now you two behave, you'll be embarrassing the Meenister!" Donald John said.

Colin had gone from pale white to a bright red in a matter of seconds. On seeing his embarrassment, everyone laughed. Everyone except Colin, that was.

"Oh…g..g..gosh!" Colin stuttered with embarrassment, growing more red by the minute. Realising how he must have looked, he too started to laugh until all five of them were in fits of laughter, although no-one was quite sure what they were laughing at.

It was Rhona herself who broke the mood by announcing, "This will never do, the mince and tatties won't cook themselves!" and the girls burst out in a fit of laughter once more.

Donald John hadn't forgotten his dram. "What a fine looking dram!" he announced by way of changing the subject as he held up his glass of whisky and looked through the glass.

"What do you say Meenister?" Colin didn't know a good whisky from a glass of Irn Bru but not wanting to upset Donald John he looked into the glass, swirled it around a few times, smelled the distinctive peaty aroma of Jura and the other Islay malts. "Yes, it's an exceptionally good dram," he pronounced, at which Donald John said, "I like a Meenister who knows a good dram when he smells one, Slainte Mhath Meenister!" and drank it down in one smooth action.

There was nothing else for it but to reply in like manner, *'what's the worst that could happen?'* Colin thought, and he downed the whisky in one gulp, but unlike Donald John's expert swig, the amber nectar slowly burned its way down inside his chest until it hit his stomach where it exploded in a burst of flavours such as Colin had never experienced before. His whole body seemed to erupt in a spasm of coughing and spluttering, sending Mhàiri and Kirsty into another fit of laughter.

"Now, now you two," their father said. "That's enough of that! The Meenister is choking on a fine dram and all you can do iss to go into a fit of the giggles!" which only served to set them off again. Donald John shook his head and said under his breath, *"What a waste of a good dram!"*

All the noise brought Rhona through from the kitchen. She saw the girls giggling, Colin having an attack of some sort and Donald John shaking his head.

"What on earth is going on in here!?" she said. "Donald John! Can you not see that the Meenister is having a fit? Away over and help him for pity's sake!"

"Aye, I was just thinking that myself," he said and went to see if he could offer assistance to the Reverend.

As she looked over at Colin, Rhona could see his eyes were streaming, he was holding his stomach and coughing violently. "Oh mercy me! Is he going to be alright Donald John?"

"Aye, he'll be fine, his dram went down the wrong way, that's all," Donald John explained.

Rhona turned to her two daughters and said sharply, "And will you two lassies stop your laughing!"

In time, everyone calmed down and Rhona called Mhàiri and Kirsty into the kitchen to set the table for tea. Shortly afterwards she called, "Ok everyone, that's the tea on the table, come and get it!"

As Donald John and Colin entered the kitchen, Rhona pointed to the chair at one end of the table and said to Colin, "Will you be sitting up there your Reverence? A special place for a special visitor. Will you put up a grace for us and thank the good Lord for all his mercies?"

"Of course," Colin agreed, "And once we are all seated, perhaps we might all join hands around the table?" This was a custom that he and his Divinity friends observed whenever they shared a meal together, they felt it united them as friends and as part of God's family.

Once they were all were seated, Colin found himself with Mhàiri on his left and Kirsty on his right side. The sisters each took a hand of Colin, looked at each other and smiled in a coy and embarrassed kind of way.

The Grace was given and they all said, 'Amen.'

As they ate and chatted, Colin felt so blessed to be sitting at a table with such a lovely family round about him.

'*Maybe one day,*' Colin mused, '*God would bless him with a happy family too,*' but that was in the hands of the good Lord.

The meal was shared and very much appreciated, especially by Colin who rarely had the pleasure of enjoying home cooked food, not only that, mince and tatties was his all time favourite meal.

Rhona and the girls cleared up while Colin and Donald John went through to the sitting room to discuss more serious issues.

"What did you think of the whisky, Meenister? Thon Jura is a grand dram, eh?" Donald John asked, hoping for Colin's approval.

"Oh ye...yes!" Colin stuttered.

"A fine dram it is indeed Donald John, just a pity it er..."

"Went down the wrong way?" Donald John said helpfully.

"Yes, .... down the wrong way – yes, that was it," Colin replied.

"Aye, just that," Donald John kindly agreed.

It was a pleasant evening as the five of them chatted their way through a number of topics such as, 'what makes a good whisky', 'how a fine sea trout compliments a good whisky' and Donald John declared that fishing with a net was the most humane way to catch a fish without putting stress on the fish - and other whisky and fish related topics.

When Donald John thought that it was time for bed, he was surprised to see that he and Colin were the only two left in the room.
Rhona and the girls had slid out an hour or so before, giving Colin a smile and a wee wave as they slipped out and off to bed.

Colin feigned a yawn and bade goodnight to Donald John who rose, saying, "Good night Meenister, sleep well."
"And yourself," replied Colin, "And may the angels watch over you and your family as you sleep."
Donald John was deeply touched and went through to his bed with a tear in his eye.
Colin slept well, even although it had been 1am and still light outside when he had gone to bed.

The next thing he knew was being wakened by the sound of Mhàiri and Kirsty bringing in a plate of hot, steaming porridge and a small cup of cream, along with a small barrel glass of whisky, all on a wooden tray.

"Father says he will be heading off to Rhua in a wee while or so," said Kirsty.

"If you would like to be ready by then," added Mhàiri.

They both giggled and ran out of the bedroom before Colin got a chance to reply.

He enjoyed his porridge and cream, got washed and dressed in haste but wasn't sure what to do with the well-intended glass of whisky. He noticed a flower in a small pot on a small table across the room, and to save upsetting Donald John and Rhona, he poured the whisky slowly into the flower pot, placed the empty glass on the tray and took the tray through to the kitchen.

"Ah, it is yourself Meenister, did you sleep well?" Rhona said as Colin entered the kitchen.

"Yes, I did and thank you for such a hearty breakfast."

"You're most welcome Meenister. Oats and barley is a healthy way to start the day, oats in the porridge and barley in the whisky. That's why we're all so healthy away up here." Lorna said without a hint of a smile.

"You'll be looking for Donald John," she continued. "He's down at the boat, he said you were just to make your way down when you are ready, the lassies will show you the way," which caused the girls to go red in the face and giggle.

"Ok, that's great," said Colin as he picked up his coat and case and made for the door. He turned and said, "Thank you so much for your hospitality Rhona, you have been very kind, may God bless you and your delightful family," and stepped out of the lovely wee croft.

Mhàiri and Kirsty were a good distance in front and shouted to Colin, "Come on Meenister, the tide will be against you if you don't hurry!"

As he strode down the path, across the road and along the shoreline, he turned for a final look at the lovely wee croft with Rhona standing at the door holding a handkerchief to her eyes as she wiped away a tear.

# Chapter 9

*"Oh mercy, it's…it's a Meenister!"*

♦

Colin looked around for the 'fine-looking boat' that his friend Iain had told him about. However, just along the shoreline, he spotted Mhàiri and Kirsty waving at him, shouting, "Over here Meenister!"

*'There must be some mistake,'* he thought. They were standing next to a small, dilapidated boat much in need of repair and more than one good lick of paint, with a rusty and outdated looking outboard engine hanging over the back of the wee boat.

As he made his way over towards the boat he saw Donald John looking out to sea and then up at the skies and he shouted, "We'll have to get a move on Meenister if we are to make it over to Rhua before the rain comes on, hurry now." Colin quickened his step and the girls came back to meet him and took his coat and case and passed them over to their father.

Donald John helped Colin into the small boat saying, "Make yourself at home Meenister," but the boat was so cluttered with fishing nets, rope and cork floats that he could hardly find a spot to sit down.

"Could we not have left the nets on the shore?" asked Colin.

"Mercy me, no!" replied Donald John, "you never know when we might spot a fine sea trout in need of protecting from the seals." Colin thought it was rather a dubious explanation but chose not to pursue it any further.

He managed to clear a small area among the nets and other fishing paraphernalia and made himself as comfortable as possible.

Mhàiri and Kirsty pushed the boat out until they were knee deep in the water. After a number of attempts, Donald John managed to coax the outboard motor into life and away they went at a great speed. Colin held on tight, closed his eyes and said a prayer for a safe passage.

The girls waved enthusiastically and then ran up

to the croft where, along with their mother, all three waved until the wee boat was well out at sea. Colin wished he was in the safety of the Croft too as Donald John opened up the throttle and the wee boat surged and bumped across the waves sending showers of spray over them both.

After about 10 minutes or so, Colin scanned the horizon, hoping to see their destination, but saw no sign of land. "I can't see Rhua yet," Colin said, thinking it was just a short hop over to Rhua. "Oh no, it's a wee bit away yet Meenister."
"How long will it take us to get over there?" Colin asked. "Och, no' long, maybe an hour or so, if the winds are with us," came the reply. Colin nearly fell into the bottom of the boat, *'An hour!?'*

He couldn't imagine another hour of this spray and continual bumping, and besides, he was beginning to feel a bit queasy.
Donald John just laughed and said, "We'll be there before you know it," and took out a hip flask from his pocket and held it up for Colin to take. "Just a wee dram to calm the nerves?" Colin could think of nothing worse than to drink

whisky at that time of the morning. Donald John laughed again and took a large swig, put the flask back in his pocket and opened up the throttle once more.

"Oh, Lord preserve us!" Colin cried out.

"I'm quite sure he will, Meenister!" Donald John agreed and began to sing the first verse of the seafarer's hymn, "For those in peril on the sea," in Gaelic, but could only remember the words of the first two verses.

Colin didn't know the Gaelic words but he certainly knew the Hymn and joined in and sang with great feeling.

They followed with the 23rd Psalm, *"The Lord is my Shepherd"* and then the 121st Psalm, *"I to the hills will lift mine eyes,"* finishing off their 'hymn-a-long,' with Psalm 100, *"All people that on earth do dwell,"* which settled Colin down and the rest of the journey went without incident.

At last, Donald John pointed across to the Port side and shouted above the waves, "Rhua ahead!" As Colin turned, he was relieved to see land not too far away. *'Thank the Lord, safe at last,'* he said to himself and a great sense of relief came over him. God was surely watching over them.

As they drew near the shoreline, Donald John cut the engine and they drifted the last few yards until they were almost alongside the small jetty where a young man who had been fishing laid down his rod and made ready to moor them to the jetty.

"Meenister, look smart! Throw the rope to the lad or we'll hit the rocks for sure!" Donald John shouted.

They had discussed this on the way over and Colin felt confident that he would manage it without any bother.

"Make quick!" Donald John said with some urgency in his voice.

"Are you remembering? The rope with the blue tape, throw it to the lad!"

Colin panicked momentarily. He had just noticed there were 3 or 4 pieces of rope, all with blue tape wrapped around the end. So, taking courage in his hand, he picked up the nearest rope and threw it over to the lad onshore, who caught it and tied it to a rusty metal ring.

Colin had chosen the correct rope. "That was a lucky shot Meenister," said Donald John smiling. Colin did not put any store in 'luck,' and replied, "There's no such thing as 'luck,' Donald John, the good Lord directed my hand as I knew he would!" Donald John wasn't convinced but was just pleased to be moored safely to the jetty without any mishap.

Donald John handed up Colin's case and coat to the lad and they both climbed up the unsteady ladder onto the small pier.

"Thank you, fear òg," *(young man)* Donald John said in the Gaelic, and before the lad could answer, he noticed Colin's Ministerial dog collar and was visibly shaken. "Oh mercy, it's…it's a Meenister!" he said.

"Aye, a man of the cloth," said Donald John sternly, "so you'd better be watching your language, none of your Rhua coarseness, now!" and he winked at Colin.

"No…no… it was just the shock of it," the young man said in his own defence.

"Aye well, mind your place, and where is Callum

McLeod? He was supposed to meet us," Donald John asked.

"I.. I.. don't know, but I was hearing that Callum and Lachie Mhór were caught at the poaching by 'PC Bookem' and the two of them were locked up in the cells," the boy answered.

To Colin's surprise Donald John was not happy. "Mercy me! What was he thinking about, being caught poaching!?" It took Colin all his time not to laugh out loud, considering Donald John's own reputation as a prolific poacher.

Donald John's indignant outburst calmed as quickly as it had flared up. "Well, pick up the Meenister's luggage and take him up to Mrs McLeod's croft, and be quick, the Meenister doesn't have all day! He is about God's business!"

"Aye Donald John, just as you say," the boy said and picked up Colin's case and indicated for him to follow.

Colin thanked Donald John and walked up the jetty with the lad. He turned to see his friend roaring off at a great rate of knots, singing the Lewis Gaelic song 'Tha thu fada bhuam' – "You are far from me."

Colin caught up with him and by way of making conversation, he asked the boy what his name was.

"Duncan Begg," he replied.

"Begg? that's not a West Highland name is it?"

"Oh aye," Duncan replied. "It's a by-name in Gaelic for 'small,' Duncan *Beck* as we would say."

"Oh right," Colin realised that Duncan was indeed quite slight in his build. Feeling awkward he quickly changed the subject by saying, "So Duncan, how do you know Donald John?"

"Oh, everyone knows Donald John in these parts. But he never hangs around very long, he knows that Bookem the bobby is after him! Aye, he's an awfa' man!" and Duncan Begg's smile broadened.

And then, completely unprompted, Duncan said, "Donald John's wife, you know, Rhona, is my Aunty, she was born on Rhua."

"Oh?" Colin said but not knowing what to say after that, he simply said, "Aye" which seemed to satisfy Duncan who nodded and replied, "Aye, well..." as they walked on.

Colin hadn't appreciated just how many meanings the simple word, 'Aye' could have.

He shook his head and thought, '*The West Highlands! What a strange and yet fascinating part of God's Kingdom.*'

Before long, they came to a small croft. "Here we are Meenister, Mrs McLeod's croft, the finest B&B on Rhua."

"Are there many B&B's on Rhua?" Colin asked.

"Mercy no, she is the only one!" Duncan Begg replied.

Colin shook his head and smiled to himself, '*Islanders!*' he thought and opened the gate.

"Oh, a wee tip for you Meenister," Duncan said in a whisper, "Don't be over-familiarising yourself with Mrs McLeod, she doesn't hold with levity and such like. A new Locum Doctor was over on the Island last year and asked if he might call her by her first name, and she tore a strip off him for being too familiar!"

"Oh right, I'll be sure not to ask her first name," Colin replied.

"Does she *have* a first name, Duncan?"

"No one knows, she will only answer to, *Mrs*

*McLeod*," replied Duncan.

"Oh well Duncan, thank you for your help, wish me well.
Into the Lion's Den," Colin said as he walked down the path and knocked on the door of Mrs McLeod's croft, the finest Bed and Breakfast in all of Rhua.

# Chapter 10

*"The BBC Home Service is forecasting storms over the next few days..."*

◆

The door opened and a dark haired, formidable looking lady stood there.

"Mrs McLeod, I presume?" said Colin with a friendly smile.

"It is," the lady answered with a glower. "And you'll be the Meenister."

"I am indeed. At your service ma'am."

"And just what do you mean by that!?" Mrs McLeod said accusingly.

"Oh...just a friendly greeting, that is all Mrs McLeod."

"Aye, well, you had better come in and wipe your feet before you do."

Colin dutifully wiped his feet on the well worn door mat, and entered the croft with some apprehension.

"That will be your room on the left," Mrs McLeod pointed to a bedroom door, and don't be thinking of wandering about the house after dark, my room is securely locked!"

Colin wasn't quite sure what she was insinuating, but 'wandering about the house after dark' certainly wasn't going to happen, he was quite sure of that.

"You'll be wanting a cup of tea I am thinking Meenister," was more of a statement than a question.

"Yes please, that would be much appreciated Mrs McLeod, I am rather parched, to say the least."

"You'll not be taking the sugar, it's the devil's way of poisoning our bodies," and she gave a slight blush at the word, 'bodies.'

"Oh... well... no thank you," Colin felt it better to abstain on this occasion even though he had a sweet tooth.

"Away through and take a seat." she said to Colin.

Mrs McLeod had a small, round table with a white doily laid on top, already positioned next to the armchair in preparation for the Meenister's visit.

Within a few minutes she came through with a tray on which was a plate of scones, straight off the girdle, two pink china side plates with matching cups, a milk jug, a small tea pot – and a matching bowl which contained a good portion of her own, home made gooseberry jam.

"Goodness me, Mrs McLeod, what a veritable feast, to be sure!"

"Och, away with you, Meenister," said Mrs McRae, blushing. Colin had made a good first impression.

"You're very young to be a Meenister, where is your Church?" Mrs McLeod inquired.
"Yes, I'm 26 years old and serving the good Lord as an assistant Minister in an old Church of Scotland in Glasgow but I'm looking for a Parish of my own," Colin responded.
"Oh, not the Free Church then?" Mrs McLeod seemed disappointed.
Changing the subject, Colin spread some gooseberry jam over the scone and asked, "Are these your own scones Mrs McLeod? They are very tasty, and the gooseberry jam is delicious too."

"Aye, Meenister, and who else's scones would they be!?" Mrs McLeod said, taking offence to the outrageous suggestion that she would pass off someone else's scones and jam as her own.

"Oh,.. well.. I.. er.. well of course… I mean.." Colin stuttered. "Yours of course Mrs McLeod, the tongue of good report has gone before you ma'am. Donald John from Coll told me about your amazing home baking skills." Colin felt a pang of guilt come over him and hoped that the good Lord would forgive him for using such false flattery.

"I believe Donald John is a relation of yours Mrs McLeod."

"Yes, and more's the pity! He is a rogue, and a poacher too!" Mrs McLeod was visibly irritated. "He's a blight on our God fearing Island!

He's wanted by the police the length and breadth of the West coast. Our own policeman, PC Bookem is run ragged with his carry-on's!"

"Bookem is an unusual name, Mrs McLeod, is that his *real* name?"

"Mercy no, he is an enthusiastic Polis-man. His motto is, *'book 'em first and ask questions later'*!"

"Oh dear, I had better watch myself while I'm here then!" Colin joked, but Mrs McLeod wasn't one for the jokes. "I should think so too! And you a Meenister!" she said in a firm voice.

He was caught off guard, so he thought it best to change the subject, and said, "Donald John tells me that your grandfather was the Minister here on Rhua many years ago."

"Yes, he was the Free Church Minister before Mr McCrimmond."

"Where do the Free Church meet?" Colin asked.

"They worship in the Church of Scotland building now. The Free Church meet at 10 o'clock, the Church of Scotland congregation meet there at 11 o'clock, and the R. C's, for all there are of them, have their services at 12.30."

"Oh goodness, how very Ecumenical!" Colin had never heard of such amity, '*it wouldn't happen in Glasgow,*' he thought to himself.

"Oh yes, we are very open on Rhua. It was Mr McMillan, the Church of Scotland Meenister who brought it about. He invited all the denominations to worship in his church and we all share the upkeep. *'It's all the same God that we worship in our own different ways,'* he used to say - that was before he passed away of course, God rest his soul."

"Yes, of course, and does it work well?"

"Oh yes Meenister, we all get on very well, for most of the time. We have our moments but Mr McCrimmond keeps us in order."

"And is the church far away?"

"Oh no, it will be only about 5 miles or so, not far to walk for a young man of the cloth such as yourself."

Colin choked as he tried to stifle a cough. "5 miles!" He would never dream of walking 5 miles unless it were on the hills of Glencoe.

"5 Miles!?" he repeated.

Mrs McLeod shook her head and said, "Och, you youngsters today, no stamina. Well, my grandfather's car is in the garage and as you are a man of the cloth, I am sure he wouldn't object to you using it, especially as it is in God's service that you are. When are you going back to the mainland?"

"Donald John is picking me up on Friday

morning. I think it all depends on the weather and the tides."

"It'll be in God's hands if you get back to the mainland anytime soon. The BBC Home Service is forecasting storms over the next few days."

"It looks nice enough today, Mrs McLeod," Colin said as he looked out of the small window.

"Aye, but it can change hour by hour out here, we'll have to wait and see."

"Aye," Colin agreed with a slight nod of his head. He was getting used to using the word, 'Aye' in different situations.

"Would you like to see the car? It's in the garage. Away out and take it for a run up to the end of the road to see what you think," Mrs McLeod suggested.

"That would be great, you're very kind Mrs McLeod. I'll pop my case in the bedroom on the way out."

"Don't you be bothering about your case, I'll lay it in your room for you when you are away out. Now off you go and I'll start preparing lunch for us. What time is your funeral?"

"3 o'clock," Colin answered.

"It's only half past 11 now so you have plenty of time," came the reply.

Colin felt that Mrs McLeod was beginning to thaw out, indeed he felt she might be developing a soft spot for him. *'Och, away with you,'* he said to himself and realised just how much he was beginning to sound like the locals. Was that a good thing? Colin wasn't so sure.

He walked round to see a tumbled down wooden garage. As he pulled the door open it came straight off its hinges and fell to the ground.

*"Oh dear, here's me just arrived and I'm demolishing the garage already!"* he said to himself.

As he peered into the darkness, his breath was fair taken away – it was a beautiful 1929 Rolls Royce Barker 2-Door Saloon Coupe in an almost good as new condition, except for a few cobwebs. He admired its beautiful lines and wire spoked wheels. The 'winged lady' on the bonnet was gleaming as if it had been polished every day since the day it was made. He suddenly realised that he had stopped breathing and inhaled with a gasp.

Who on earth would have thought that such a car would be found in an old derelict garage on a remote Scottish Island?

He opened the door and slid onto the soft leather seat, pushing back into the seat to feel its luxury. But there was something amiss, what was it? As Colin breathed in the smell of the leather upholstery, he detected a strong and rather unpleasant odour. What could it be?

Was it fish? Surely not.

He walked round to the back and opened the boot to find two lobster creels, some fishing nets, a rope and some fish scales on the plush carpeting.

He couldn't imagine the God fearing Mrs McLeod running a Salmon poaching racket.

Very fishy, very fishy indeed.

# Chapter 11

*"Singing to God in his own tongue…"*

◆

Colin went back into the kitchen and said excitedly, "Oh Mrs McLeod, it's beautiful! Are you sure it's alright for me to take it out for a run?"

"Of course, Meenister, the keys are hanging on a nail behind the back door. Why not run over to the Church to get your bearings for later?

If you go to the top of the road, turn left, and go down to the foot of the hill and then turn right, keep going and you'll see the church further down the road. But don't be too long though, lunch will be ready in an hour."

"I'll be back in good time, unless I get lost," he said as he hastily left the room.

He picked up his hat from his room on the way by and hurried out to the car.

Soon he was cautiously pulling out onto the road and then slowly up to the top of the road. The car was purring beautifully.

As he gained confidence, so his speed increased

and following Mrs McLeod's directions, he soon found himself pulling up outside the Rhua Parish Church of Scotland.

If he had been a betting man, which of course he most certainly was not, he would be quite sure that there would be another church building somewhere on the Island, one that was lying dormant.

During the time of the Disruption in the mid 1800's the Free Church built their own churches across the highlands and islands of Scotland, often near a Church of Scotland. Over the years, one usually thrived while the other fell silent.

Colin entered the church by a side door and startled a cleaning lady who was sitting in the kitchen drinking a cup of tea. "Oh, excuse me," Colin said, "I wasn't expecting to meet anyone."

"Oh, come away in Meenister," she said, "We were just taking a wee break, but we'd better get back to work, there's a funeerial service here later today."

"Yes, I know," Colin said to the cleaner and the elderly gentleman who has just appeared at the inner door to the church.

"Oh of course! You'll be the Meenister from Glaschu, dear Mrs McGillivray's grandson, am I right?" said the elderly gentleman.
"Let me introduce myself, John McRae, I'm the Presenter, I'll be leading the singing this afternoon."
"So, you are the organist?" Colin asked.
"Indeed, I am not! There is no organ in this church! It's the devil's instrument! I 'present' the Psalms Meenister," replied John McRae. "I sing the first line and the congregation follow - and we sing in harmony to the Good Lord. Have you not heard the Gaelic Psalms being sung?"
"Sorry John, no I haven't, it sounds, well, interesting."

"What Psalms are you wanting to sing at the funeral Meenister?" asked John.
"Well er… I was planning on singing, 'All things bright and beautiful' to the tune Royal Oak, and 'I heard the voice of Jesus say,' to the Robert Vaughan Williams tune, Kingsfold.

"Oh mercy no Meenister, no one would know those fancy new Hymns, we only sing the Psalms here."

Colin knew that these were far from, 'fancy new hymns' indeed both were written around 1850 with even older tunes, but rather than upset John the Presenter he said, "Oh right, so what do you suggest?"

"Well, we usually sing the 23rd Psalm and Psalm 121, they'll all know those."

Colin smiled and said, "In Glasgow, the traditional churches use the '23rd Psalm' and 'Abide with me' at all the funerals, we call them, *'The Co-operative double!'*

"Well," John said indignantly, "Singing biblical Psalms to our Lord are still important to the God fearing people here on the Islands!"

Colin hadn't meant to upset John and apologised profusely.

Taking the line of least resistance, Colin agreed to John's suggestion.

When you say, *'they'll all knows them,'* John, how

many people should we expect at the service?"

"Oh mercy, the church will be full Meenister!"

At which Colin went visibly pale.

"Full? Gosh I was expecting a dozen or so, after all, she has no family here."

"Maybe not but she was well known on the Island and held in the highest esteem. And besides that, we see ourselves as one family here on Rhua," John said. "And we support each other in difficult times."

"Would you like to go into the church Meenister?" asked the cleaning lady.

"Oh yes, that's very kind of you …er… I'm sorry, what is your name, how rude of me not to ask sooner."

"I am Catherine, Catherine Cameron, John here is my uncle," she said with a nod to John the Presenter.

"Oh, that's good…. well, yes, I'd love to go into the Sanctuary thank you." Catherine led Colin in to the church, followed by John.

Colin was taken aback at just how austere and

stark the church was, no posters, no Women's Guild tapestries or flowers. Not at all like the churches that he was used to. He later found out that it was stop the worshippers from being distracted during their time of worship.

"So, no organ, you say, John?"

"No indeed, Meenister," John said firmly. "We wouldn't countenance such a thing as an organ! We sing nothing but the Psalms."

"And beautiful it is," said Catherine.

"Yes, indeed Catherine, singing praises to God in His own tongue!" John said proudly.

"Aye, just that," Catherine agreed.

Colin could see it was a sensitive matter so he walked over to the Pulpit stairs and climbed to the top where he surveyed the Sanctuary from his lofty position.

To lighten the mood Colin said loudly and with a smile, "Nearer my God to Thee!" and looked up to the ceiling. He was expecting a jovial response but it fell on deaf ears.

After a short awkward silence in which John the

Presenter shook his head slowly and Catherine wondered what was going on, Colin asked no-one in particular, "Is the service at 3 o'clock?"

He knew it was 3pm but felt he should change the subject.

"Aye," Catherine and John the Presenter said together.

"Ok, that's good, thank you. I'll be back about 2.30, I look forward to seeing you both later, and thank you for your help and advice."

He descended to floor level and made his way out of the sombre atmosphere of the church and into his luxurious mode of transport.

He felt a hint of guilt, as he, a man of God, was indulging himself in the earthly extravagance of such a luxurious motor car.

He turned the ignition key and heard the gentle purr of the engine and his feelings of guilt dissolved as he said to himself, *'If the Good Lord didn't want me to drive such a beautiful car, He would have left an old bicycle in Mrs McLeod's garage!'*

Feeling more justified, he drove back to the croft.

"How did you get on at the Church, Meenister?" Mrs McLeod asked.

"Oh fine, I met John McRae the Presenter and young Catherine Cameron."

"Oh John! What a wonderful voice he has! He leads us in the singing of the Psalms on the Sabbath. Never was there a Presenter with such a heavenly voice.

He also presents for the Free Church too. He sings praises to God in His own tongue!"

"Yes, that's just what John McRae said.

What delights do we have for lunch Mrs McLeod?"

"I have a wee treat for you Meenister, seeing as you are doing God's work this afternoon, a nice piece of Poached Salmon."

Colin almost fell off his chair as he thought of eating a meal that was taken illegally.

"By... 'poached'.... Do you mean...?"

"Oh, mercy no, Meenister! It's been poached in milk with baby onions from our very own garden, a special treat! Imagine you thinking that I would give a man of the cloth a fish which was taken dishonestly!" Mrs McLeod shook her head.

"My apologies Mrs McLeod, I didn't mean to suggest….."
"No need to apologise Meenister, my husband has the contacts and he assures me it's all above board."
"Your husband!?" Colin was surprised to hear that there was a *Mr* McLeod.

"Yes, my husband Callum, he is well known on the island and hereabouts."

Colin could hear the sound of pennies dropping. "Do you mean Callum McLeod the p…" and he held himself back from saying, *'do you mean Callum McLeod the Poacher?'* but continued, "Callum McLeod the …er…the local er…piper ?"
"Yes, that's him, but he hasn't played the pipes for a long time – he is too busy these days. Why, have you heard of him?" said Mrs McLeod.
"Oh yes Mrs McLeod, I think I have heard his name mentioned somewhere."
Colin thought, *'According to the young man fishing*

at the jetty, was it not Callum McLeod and Lachie Mór who were caught poaching and locked up in the local police station?'

Perhaps there was some mistake, but in his heart Colin felt sure there was more to it than meets the eye.

'Well, well,' Colin thought to himself, 'who would have believed it, Callum McLeod, the local Poacher was the prim and proper Mrs McLeod's husband!

Perhaps that might explain the fish scales in the boot of the car!'

His thoughts were interrupted when Mrs McLeod proudly laid his lunch on the table.

"Mmmm, that looks good Mrs McLeod," Colin said, thankful to be able to divert the conversation.

"Thank you Meenister, now eat up, you have serious responsibilities to attend to."

"Aye," replied Colin before saying a Grace and tucking into his lunch of boiled potatoes, onions and Poached Salmon, poached in milk.

He smiled at the irony.

# Chapter 12

*"It's from an old Gaelic blessing – 'Cuiridh mi*
*clach air do chàrn' which means 'When you are gone,*
*I'll put a stone on your cairn…"*

❖

After lunch he went through to his room, sat on
the bed and offered up a prayer, asking for
strength, composure and compassion, and that
through his service of handing his dear
Grandmother back into the Lord's safe keeping –
he might give God all the glory, and comfort to
the bereaved.

He read through his notes for the Service,
changing a word or two here and there, then
opened his case and took out his Bible, turning to
Isaiah 40 : 28 - 31, *'Do you not know, have you not*
*heard? The Lord, the eternal God, creator of earth's*
*farthest bounds, does not grow weary or grow faint.*
*His understanding cannot be fathomed. He gives*
*strength to the weary and increases power to the*
*weak…'*
Suitably composed and strengthened, Colin put
his black Geneva gown over his arm and his Bible

and notes into his small case and made his way through to the kitchen where Mrs McLeod was just putting the kettle on. "Will you be having a cup of tea before you go, Meenister?"

"Not just now thank you, Mrs McLeod."

"What about a wee dram? It might give more power to your sermon. Rev McCrimmond always takes a wee dram before Preaching."

"I like to have a clear head, Mrs McLeod," Colin replied.

"The Rev McCrimmond says it *clears* his head!" was Mrs McLeod's reply.

"Well, I had better be going, I like to be in good time," Colin said as he moved toward the door.

"Of course, Meenister, and may God's blessing be upon you."

"Thank you Mrs McLeod, I really appreciate your kindness." He was sure he saw the righteous Mrs McLeod give a slight blush. "Och, away with you now! I'm old enough to be your mother!" she said with a coy smile.

'More like *grand*-mother,' Colin thought, but then

immediately chastised himself.

"You're a gem, Mrs McLeod, any man would be honoured to be your husband. Your Callum is truly blessed!" Colin said as he walked out of the door for fear of any further embarrassment.

*'The poor boy is fair smitten,'* Mrs McLeod said to herself, *'I suppose I have aged well, the good Lord has been to kind to me, right enough.'*
As she turned to say goodbye to her young admirer she tripped on the edge of the worn door mat, landing unceremoniously on her rear end on the kitchen floor - and she remembered a saying her mother often used, *'Pride comes before a fall.'*

When he drove up to the Church, Colin felt a certain amount of apprehension. Butterflies were flying around his stomach as he thought of a church full of mourners, all of whom actually *knew* his grandmother, whereas he had only met her once or twice when he was a young.
"Oh well, the good Lord is with me," Colin said to reassure himself.

As he arrived at the Church, he was taken aback by the number of people who were standing around chatting. As he got out of the car the conversations stopped and all eyes were turned towards him.

He smiled and hurried through the side door and into the kitchen where John McRae and young Catherine Cameron were waiting.

"Goodness me!" Colin said, "What a gathering outside, reminiscent of the feeding of the 5,000!"

"Aye, they have come to see the new Meenister!" Catherine said shyly.

"Gosh," was all Colin could think to say, followed by, "Goodness me... I had better go through and get my notes arranged," and he walked through to the Sanctuary.

Once more he was amazed at the number of people who were already in the church.

The hubbub became a tense silence as Colin walked in and went up to the Pulpit. He smiled, nodded and gave a half wave, then realised that he must have looked a bit odd, more especially when he heard one lady saying, "Aww it's a shame, he's just a boy."

Colin smiled nervously and scurried back into the kitchen.

"Don't worry," John McRae said with a smile "The natives are friendly!"
"Thank the Lord for that!" replied Colin.

"I think a hot cup of tea is called for," said Catherine pouring out black tea into a large mug. "Will you take milk, Meenister?"
"Okay then Catherine, thank you, but just a half cup please."
 She handed him a mug and he took a long gulp of tea. He nearly brought it all back up again as he said, "Goodness Catherine, the tea is very strong!" and started to cough.
John the Presenter smiled.

As Colin chatted and sipped at his cup of tea, he thought it had a peaty taste, *'Perhaps it's the Island water?'* he thought. Little did he know that Catherine had added something a little stronger than water into his tea.

A warm glow came over him and he felt buoyed up with a strange new confidence.

Soon the church bells rang out, announcing that the service was about to begin, and the people filed into Church.

Colin put down his mug, John McRae offered up a short prayer and led Colin through to the sanctuary where he gave the Service of his life.

So eloquent, so meaningful and erudite.

Colin closed his eyes and thanked God for giving him the strength and confidence needed to conduct such a difficult service. Catherine, however, was sure it was her 'special' cup of tea. Whatever it was, it certainly worked!

At the end of the Service, he asked the congregation to stand for the Benediction, and when he indicated that they should be seated, they remained standing and began to clap, slowly and hesitantly at first but then with gusto.

Colin looked down and saw a lovely lady in a wheelchair clapping for all her worth, beaming from ear to ear.

As he caught her eye, she smiled and gave him the thumbs up sign.

"Oh mercy!" he heard John the Presenter say, "What will the Elders say?"
He then noticed the Elders, who had been seated in a 'pen' beneath the Pulpit, facing the congregation, were standing and clapping too, so John smiled and joined in!

Colin stood there saying, "Oh goodness me, gosh..." John the Presenter could see Colin's embarrassment and came up and led him down from the Pulpit, up the central isle and through to the vestibule inside the front door of the church where his grandmothers' coffin had been throughout the service. "Well done Meenister!" John said. "There is no doubt that the Spirit was in you today! This church has never seen a service like that, you did your dear Grandmother proud! She is with the Angels now, and there will be rejoicing in Heaven tonight for sure!"

As the Elders came out of the church, a small group of them lifted Mrs McGillivray's coffin on to their shoulders and carried her down to the shore where another group of Elders took the coffin and walked about a mile along the well worn path by the shoreline, with the mourners following on.

There was excited talk about Colin's funeral service. "Aye," said one lady, "He's the Meenister for us, and he's good looking too!"
"Mary!" another lady said. "Show some reverence! Mind you, he's a smasher alright!" and the ladies giggled, bringing a grim glower of reproach from the Elder who was walking alongside them.

As the group rounded the point, the small path turned left and up to the cemetery gates where two Elders stood, one either side of the gate. It looked as if they were guarding the very gates of heaven – and in a way, they were.
Before proceeding up to the cemetery, a third group, made up of the more senior Elders, took over and carried Mrs McGillivray to her final

resting place, next to her dear husband, Jimmack, affectionally known as. 'the Pilot.'

Colin had asked Reverend McCrimmond to conduct the short Interment service as he had been a good and faithful visitor and friend to the McGillivray's over many years.

Once the brief interment service was finished, a hand bell was rung and each mourner came forward and threw a handful of soil on top of the coffin.

Reverend McCrimmond whispered, "Earth to Earth," at every handful.

Colin was struck by the sincerity and the solemn dignity which each mourner had displayed when taking their part.

As they left the cemetery, each person picked up a small stone and placed it on a cairn which was just outside the gates.

"Why are they doing that?" Colin asked one of the Elders who was walking beside him.

"It's a token of remembrance. Our ancestors have been doing it for centuries, look."

The Elder pointed to a number of cairns which were scattered along the shoreline.

"It's from an old Gaelic blessing – 'Cuiridh mi clach air do chàrn,' which means, 'When you are gone, I will put a stone on your cairn to remember you.' We give our dear departed ones a final blessing as we leave them in the safe hands of the Almighty, and then we leave a stone to remind them that they are not forgotten here on earth.

It stems from the days when, after a battle had been fought, a cairn or pile of stones, would be raised in memory of those who had fallen. As the years went on, locals would add a stone to the cairn every time they passed by. It was their way of acknowledging their fallen kinsmen and of preserving their memories – and we still do that today for those among us who pass on to eternal rest."

As they walked back to the church, Colin said to Reverend McCrimmond, "That was a lovely

Committal and very sincere, thank you, very different from anything I am used to seeing."

"Yes, it's our tradition Colin. You'll have noticed that the women are present – in most of the Islands the women don't come to the graveside but it's always been our custom on Rhua for them to pay their respects along with the men. The Holy Scriptures tell us that, *"There is neither Jew nor Greek, there is neither slave nor free, there is no male and female, for you are all one in Christ Jesus."*

"Absolutely, Mr McCrimmond, absolutely. I couldn't agree more," said Colin.

"A group of ladies will come over tomorrow to tend to the grave and tidy things up." Reverend McCrimmond explained. "No-one asks or tells them to, they just want to make it nice for dear Martha."

Colin walked the rest of the way back to the church in silent contemplation and thought *'How kind and caring these people are.'*

As he made his way to the car, a large number of

people came over to compliment him on such a meaningful and comforting funeral service.

It was all very embarrassing, so much so that for an instant he felt like a celebrity, but then he remembered that many years ago his dear mother had told him of the saying, *"A man wrapped up in himself, makes a very small parcel,"* and so he shook himself out of it and drove off down the hill to the Kinlochmhor village hall where the Wake of his dear Grandmother would shortly take place.

# Chapter 13

*"The Wake…"*

◆

As he arrived at the village hall, he was met by a large group of people who were very enthusiastic about his service. "Oh Meenister, what a wonderful service," one said, "If only we had a Meenister like you here on Rhua, the Kirk would be full every Sunday!"

"Oh well …. gosh.. I don't know about that…" Colin mumbled awkwardly. "You are very kind…gosh…" as he wrestled his way through and into the hall.

He was confronted by a beehive of activity. Waitresses were bustling left and right with plates of sandwiches, tables were being laid and the buffet was looking resplendent with all sorts of food, interspersed by a large Poached *(literally)* Salmon.

*'That rascal Callum McLeod has been busy!'* Colin thought to himself and smiled.

As he stood and looked around, a noticeable buzz

of excitement could be heard and felt around the room. "Oh, it's the Meenister!" someone said, and an enthusiastic applause started. Colin didn't know where to look, but then he heard a male voice shouting, "Colin, Colin, over here!" It was the Reverend McCrimmond, the Free Church Minister, beckoning Colin to join him over at the top table.

Colin kept his head low as he made his way over to a vacant seat that the Reverend McCrimmond had kept for him. "Safety in numbers, eh?" Reverend McCrimmond said with a smile.

"Gosh, yes.. I mean, gosh!" Colin was so embarrassed by the outpouring of admiration and gratitude, that he didn't know what to say.

Reverend McCrimmond handed Colin a glass of whisky and said, "Here, take this, a drop of 'uisge beatha' (*the water of life*) it will do you good." Colin downed it in one.

After the applause had died down one of the ladies noticed that Colin was coughing and his face was going red. "Mercy me," she said loudly, "The Meenister is choking on something!" and some of the ladies ran over to help him.

"It's alright, thank you, something went down the wrong way," Colin spluttered.

Rev McCrimmond smiled and thought, *'So, he's not a whisky man eh? He'll be no match for an old hand at the drams such as myself!'*

He patted Colin's back saying, "Never you mind, it happens to the best of us, you'll be fine."

Colin gathered his thoughts and realised that the room had fallen silent. "What's happening Mr McCrimmond?" Colin asked.

"They're waiting for you to open the proceedings by giving up a Grace."

"O yes, of course, em.. Let us bow our heads as we give thanks to the good Lord for His provision to us." All heads went down as Colin delivered the Grace, and everyone in the room said, "Amen."

Colin continued, "And now I would like to invite Reverend McCrimmond to offer up a prayer."

Despite the very short notice, the experienced Reverend McCrimmond stood and delivered a long prayer beginning with, *"Oh Lord, we gather here as sinners in your sight..."* and continued for over 5 minutes in a similar vein. Some of the young waitresses, mostly teenagers, looked and smiled at each other, bowing their heads low when they saw that Colin was watching them.

After the prayer, one of the ladies came out from the kitchen, rapped on a table with a spoon and said, "May I take this opportunity to welcome the Reverend Meenister into our village hall for the first time." Someone shouted, "And I hope it won't be his last time!" which prompted a great cheer.

"As I was saying," the lady from the kitchen continued. "As I was saying, ..er..what *was* I saying?" much to the amusement of all present.

She took out a crumpled piece of paper from the pocket in her pinny and continued, "Oh yes, welcome Meenister and I am sure that I speak on behalf of us all when I say how much we appreciated your lovely and meaningful service for our dear friend, Martha McGillivray, your dear grandmother." (*There was another cheer*).
"She was well thought of and respected here on

Rhua and you handed her back to her Maker with great dignity.

I am sure that none of us here will forget you or your service.

And may I also remind you that our Parish Church is currently vacant." (*Yet another cheer went up*).

"And now, each table will go up to the buffet one after the other, in order, while I and the girls will serve the top table. Eat up!" and she went back into the kitchen while one of the older girls organised the waitresses in their duties at the top table.

'*All very organised,*' Colin thought. He was particularly impressed by the slightly older waitress who seemed to go about her duties efficiently and had a lovely, warm smile.

"Who is the young lady that's organsing the waitresses, Mr McCrimmond?" asked Colin. "Oh, that's Lorna MacDonald, her father has the Emporium in the village. She works with him in the shop.

All the boys are chasing after her, but she is fly and manages to give them the slip."

Throughout the evening, Colin would occasionally look her way, and he noticed that as she went about her duties, she would often glance over at him, only to quickly avert her eyes and blush whenever their eyes met.

Rev McCrimmond was good company and the evening went well as two young sisters sang Gaelic songs. Gaelic poems were recited and an Eightsome Reel and a Gay Gordons were danced to the music of 'the band,' which was a lone bag-piper.

The conversation came round to the Church and the two congregations on the Island. "How does that work, Mr McCrimmond?" Colin asked.

"Well, we are, of course, two separate congregations but there is much overlap. Everybody on the Island knows everybody else. Sometimes the Church of Scotland people turn up to the Free Church Service and vice versa, which is strange because I take both services and they are both the very same service, well. more or less. I may use a little less 'fire and brimstone' at the Church of Scotland services," he laughed.

"You mean that you give the same service to both congregations each Sunday but at different times?" Colin was puzzled.
"Aye, the Free Church service is at 10 o'clock and the Church of Scotland Service is at 11. And John MacRae Presents the same Psalms at both services."

"But why not just have the one service on a Sunday morning, especially as it is the same service?"
"Oh mercy, no!" said Mr McCrimmond. The 'Free Kirkers' would never approve of that!"

"But it's the *same* service!" Colin was struggling to understand the logic of it.
"Aye, just that," said Mr McCrimmond by way of explanation.
Then he continued, "The Church of Scotland Meenister passed on to greater glory about 10

years ago and I have been taking both services ever since. So, if a new Church of Scotland Meenister should ever come here to Minister to that congregation, I would go back to Ministering to my own congregation."

"Could that happen?" asked Colin.

"Oh aye, that's the agreement with the Church of Scotland offices in Edinburgh. Only we have had no applications in the 10 years! Why do you ask, are you thinking of applying yourself?" Mr McCrimmond said with a smile.

"Oh no, no, not at all, goodness me no!" and he looked up and saw Lorna smiling at him. "Good grief... er... um...no...well..." and he blushed profusely.

Mr McCrimmond was reminded of the words of Queen Gertrude in Shakespeare's, 'Hamlet,' *'Methinks thou doth protest too much!'*

As the evening wore on, the conversation drifted from one topic to another, while the ladies in the kitchen kept a constant flow of glasses of whisky to the two Ministers – keeping a tally as to who was drinking the most.

Mr McCrimmond seemed to be slightly ahead but was showing signs that he might fall off his chair at any minute! Whereas Colin drank steadily and showed no indication of any side effects at all.

By about 10 o'clock it was neck and neck with Mr McCrimmond refusing a final dram with the excuse that he had to 'be somewhere' in the morning, while Colin was feeling no effects whatsoever.

He was surprised at himself but the whisky was good and it went down so smoothly. His good friend Iain McDougal would be proud of him.

Many eyes in the hall were on the two Ministers, counting dram for dram. Some of the locals were running a sweep on who would drink the most.

At around 10.30pm, there was a loud crash and Mr McCrimmond slid off of his chair and slipped majestically under the table, like a Galleon in full sail slowly sinking beneath the waves.

Colin looked down at Mr McCrimmond, raised his glass and said, "Slainte!" *(Slanj)* and knocked back his final dram of the evening.

A great cheer went up. Colin wondered what the cheer was for but everyone else knew.
Lorna looked over at him and smiled the biggest smile. Then she gave him the thumbs up and a most obvious wink.

"Oh gosh!" said Colin and blushed, which made Lorna smile even more.

# Chapter 14

*"Lorna, get your hands off of the Meenister*
*this very minute!..."*

◆

It was Thursday morning and Colin woke early. He drew the curtains back and saw that there were black clouds overhead. It looked like Mrs McLeod was right, it was going to be a stormy day.

He rose, washed, dressed and went through to the kitchen where Mrs McLeod was stirring the porridge.

"Good morning Mrs McLeod, it looks like your prediction of rain was correct. It's pretty black out there," and as if on cue, the heavens opened and the rain came down, heavier than Colin had ever seen before.

"Would you be taking a drive into the village today, Meenister?" Mrs McLeod enquired with a smile.

"The village? I hadn't really thought about it, but I suppose I might take a look around the shops."

"That won't take you very long, but Mr MacDonald's 'Emporium' is worth taking a look in, you never know what you might find there," Mrs MacLeod said helpfully.

*'Wasn't it the Emporium that Mr McCrimmond had said that the pretty waitress worked?'* Colin thought. What was Mrs McLeod getting at? Did she know something? But how could she?

"Oh yes, the Emporium, I'd forgotten about that, I might have a look in there if I have the time." Colin knew he wasn't fooling Mrs McLeod.


"Here's your porridge Meenister," she said giving him a smile as she laid down a tray with a bowl of porridge, a cup of cream and a wee dram in front of him.

"Ah, oats and barley, a good, healthy breakfast. This will set me up for the day, Mrs McLeod."

"Aye just that Meenister.

I hear that yourself and Mr McCrimmond got on well," said Mrs McLeod. "Did you take a dram at all?"

"Yes, Mrs McLeod, maybe one or two to be sociable," Colin replied.

Mrs McLeod smiled to herself and carried on washing the dishes in the sink, not wanting to let on that she knew exactly what had happened.

After breakfast Colin thought he would take a drive into the village, but before that he had his morning prayer time to complete, so he went through to his room and read a passage or two of Scripture, spent a short time in silent contemplation and put up a prayer. Now he was ready to face the day.

He said goodbye to Mrs McLeod and drove down to the village.

It was not unlike many remote Highland and Island villages. There was only a handful of shops, most of which doubled up on their services.

There was McPhail's, a small garage that had a hand cranked petrol pump outside, but also sold jam and home bakes made daily by Mrs McPhail. There was an empty shop which had been a

Pottery but through dearth of tourists and a lack of interest by the locals, had been closed for some time by the look of it.

Next to that there was also a small shop which went under the name of, 'Mr Ali's Convenience Shop' which sold groceries as well as coal, logs paraffin and dungarees. Mr Ali spoke Gaelic as fluent as the locals, it was good for business.

There was a small Post Office, once painted Red, but like a number of the shops and other buildings in the village, was much in need of a serious lick of paint.

A rather grand looking Kinlochmhor Hotel stood across the road from the Post Office. It was faded and had seen better days, an echo of the past when the rich and famous Victorians would visit Rhua while on their 'Grand Tour' of the Highlands and Islands of Scotland.

On the corner was a Haberdashery which had Mannequins in the window, dressed in tweeds and tartan clothing, looking like actors from a black and white film of a bygone era.

Above the front window was painted the name, HARROLDS EMPORIUM in green and gold lettering which was reminiscent of a certain 'posh shop' in London.

On closer inspection it actually said, HARROLD's but the L was in smaller print and barely readable. So this was the 'famous Emporium' that Colin had been told about.

He walked past it two or three times before finally summoning up the courage to go inside.

As he opened the door a small bell which was fixed above the door, gave an unusually loud 'ding' that made Colin jump, which ruined the cool and collect entrance he had hoped to make.

The bell brought a small man bustling out from the back of the shop.

"Oh Meenister, how honourable we are to have the likes of yourself in our humble establishment," he said with a slight bow.

"Look everyone!  it's the Meenister!' he said as he fluttered around the shop waving his arms excitedly.

Three ladies who were looking at the fabrics turned and eyed Colin up and down.

"Mmmm he's a bit young to be a Meenister," one said.

"Aye," another whispered. "But he has the good looks, like a young Harry Lauder!" and the ladies covered their mouths and giggled excitedly.

"My name is Harrold, Harrold MacDonald, and this…" the man said he stretched out his arms… "…this, is my 'World Famous Emporium!"

Colin looked around and saw a rather shabby, outdated premises, *'hardly an 'Emporium,'* he thought.

"And there is more out in the back. That's where I keep my 'delicacies' as I like to call them. Come and see for yourself."

It was only slightly better. There were a number of old china figurines, 'wally dugs' as they called them in Glasgow. Two life sized mannequins stood in the corner which were labelled, 'Highland Gentleman with Lady in Tartan.'

There were rolls of tartan and tweed and a large number of dusty boxes stacked up, as well as various items of ladies clothing, all of which looked well out of date and out of fashion.

He looked around but there was no sign to of the lovely Lorna.

"Oh yes, Mr MacDonald," Colin said, "it's… um…. very nice." The ladies had followed them through and looked at each other, one of them said quietly, "Imagine telling a fabrication, and him a man of the cloth too!" And the ladies tutted at the very thought of it.

Colin was beginning to get a bit flustered, being well out of his comfort zone – when he heard a voice say, "Now don't you be bothering the Meenister with your delicacies Father!" It was Harrold MacDonald's daughter, Lorna, the pretty waitress from the previous evening. Colin's heart skipped a beat.

It was her morning off but word had got round the village that the Meenister was seen going into the Emporium and Lorna remembered that she might have left something in the back of the shop and so hurried along to pick it up.

Colin was rendered speechless for a few seconds. Never had he seen such a beautiful young woman. Her eyes were pastel blue, the colour of a cornflower, and her golden hair seemed to shimmer like the fields of barley in the breeze of a summer's day.

Her smile made him go weak at the knees, literally, so much so that he had to hold on to one of the mannequins.

He suddenly felt light headed and thought he was about to faint, but then realised that the mannequin had began to topple, and both Colin and the 'Highland Lady in Tartan' crashed to the floor in a very undignified manner.

Lorna giggled, the ladies tut-tutted and Mr MacDonald jumped back. Colin felt very foolish as he lay there tangled in the mannequin's Tartan skirt.

"Oh Gosh.. I'm ...er.. so... er... gosh... forgive me I...er... oh dear!" was all he could manage to say.

"Don't you be worrying yourself Meenister," a warm, gentle voice said, "here, let me help you up." Lorna took his arm and in trying to get up

Colin had managed to inadvertently put his arm around Lorna's waist which caused Mr MacDonald to protest loudly.

"Meenister please take your arm away from my daughter's waist! And Lorna, get your hands off of the Meenister this very minute!"
Colin was beyond embarrassed but Lorna couldn't stop giggling.
Their feet got tangled in a roll of tartan cloth and the two of them tumbled down onto the floor, much to the annoyance of Mr MacDonald.
The ladies in the shop thought it was bordering on debauchery with one of them saying, "Well I neffer, and him a Meenister too!" and the three of them walked indignantly out of the shop.

"Oh dear," Colin said once he had composed himself. "I am so sorry, "I didn't mean to... I mean I would never dream of doing such a thing... oh dear!"
But Lorna smiled coyly and said, "Never mind Meenister, we've given the village something to talk about if nothing else!"

Colin suddenly realised that he still had his arm around Lorna's waist, and he also realised that she didn't seem too anxious for him to remove it.

"Oh gosh!" said Colin. "Whatever will you think of me?" and he removed his arm.
He felt he might fall through the floor when she replied in a whisper, "Don't be worrying Meenister, I rather liked it."

"Oh right… okay, yes, well...." he stuttered. They both laughed but Lorna's father was certainly not amused, which seemed to encourage the pair to laugh even more.
Colin was smitten there and then – and from all appearances, the feeling was reciprocated.

Lorna and Colin chatted away like long lost friends and after a while Lorna asked, "Meenister, are you some kind of secret agent?" with a mischievous smile.
Colin was puzzled, "A Secret Agent?"

"Well, it's just that we have been talking away for some time now, and I still don't know your real name – is it a secret or is it just, 'Meenister'?" She said with a playful smile.

"Oh yes... gosh... of course, it's Colin, Colin Campbell," he answered.

"Well then Colin Campbell, it might be better if we don't tell my father your surname just yet, what with him being a MacDonald.

You know, the 'massacre of Glencoe' and all that!" Lorna suggested.

"Oh right," agreed Colin. "But that was such a long time ago."

"Aye, but folks in the Highlands and Islands have the long memories!"

He wasn't sure if Lorna was teasing him but whatever she was doing, he was thoroughly enjoying it.

"So, what are you doing with yourself today?" Lorna asked.

"Oh, just looking around your beautiful island."

"You will not have seen much, what with the funeral yesterday and the stormy weather today," Lorna replied.

"You're right, but I thought I'd take a drive around this afternoon, I don't suppose......?"

"Well, as it happens, I am off this afternoon and if you wouldn't mind, perhaps I could show you around? We have some beautiful scenery and historical sites too, what do you think?" asked Lorna.

Trying not to appear too keen, Colin said in a nonchalant voice, "Yes, that sounds like a good idea." But what he really wanted to say was, *'YES! YES! if it means I can spend more time with you!'*

"Would it suit you pick me up outside the shop about 1.30?" Lorna suggested.
"That will be great!" said Colin with just a little too much enthusiasm. Lorna smiled and said, "Okay then, see you at 1.30 Colin Campbell."
"Great! I look forward to it," he replied, again, a little too loudly.

Colin left the shop thinking, *'Gosh, a date! Well, sort of a date! Was I too keen?'*

Lorna went over to her father, gave him a hug and asked, "Father, can I have the afternoon off, can I? Pleeease......"

# Chapter 15

*"All the curtains were closed and the mirrors covered, as was the custom when someone had passed away…"*

◆

Colin drove back to Mrs McLeod's on a cloud, singing, *'Onward Christian Soldiers'* at full volume.

At the croft, he greeted Mrs McLeod with a cheery, "What a fine day Mrs McLeod, the sun certainly shines on the righteous!"

She looked out of the kitchen window and saw only dark clouds and heavy rain. "Aye," she smiled. "What did you think of the village, Meenister?"

"Oh, it was very nice Mrs McLeod, but I think it would benefit from a lick of paint here and there."

"Did you find time to go into Mr MacDonald's Emporium?" Mrs McLeod asked mischievously.

"Oh, the Emporium? Yes, I did pop in for a look around as you suggested," replied Colin, hoping she wouldn't press the matter, but Mrs McLeod wasn't going to give up that easily.

"Did you meet anyone there Meenister?"

"Oh, yes, some of the ladies of the village. Oh, and Mr MacDonald of course, quite a character. I particularly enjoyed his *delicacies* department.' He crossed his fingers - the good Lord would understand.

"Was there anyone else there?" Mrs McLeod was an expert at the cross examinations.

"Oh, yes, I nearly forgot, his daughter was there too, er… now, what was her name…?"

"That would be Lorna, Meenister."

"Oh right, Lorna, yes, that was it." Colin was no match for Mrs McLeod' interrogational skills.

"She kindly offered to show me around the Island this afternoon, wasn't that kind of her Mrs McLeod?"

"Yes, very kind Meenister," and she smiled to herself, sensing that the gossips were going to have a field day with this once it gets out, if it hadn't already.

Colin hummed, *'O for a thousand tongues to sing my great Redeemer's praise'* as he went through to his bedroom where he sat reading from his King James Bible.

"Lunch in 15 minutes Meenister," Mrs McLeod shouted through to Colin.
"That's grand Mrs McLeod, I'll be through just shortly – I'm just finishing off Ruth."
Before Mrs McLeod could say a word, Colin added "The Book of Ruth, you know, the Humble gleaner, she married Boaz in the Old Testament."
"Thank the good Lord for that!" Mrs McLeod said, rolling her eyes. *"Meenisters today! They weren't like that in my day!"* she thought to herself.

Lunch was a plate of vegetable Broth, thickened with an abundance of barley, and a bowl of boiled potatoes with their skins on.
"A veritable feast Mrs McLeod," Colin said. "You are certainly doing me proud, thank you so much."
"Och, away with you," Mrs McLeod blushed. "Is it not just a plate of broth?"
"It is, Mrs McLeod, but it's the love and care that goes into making it that are the special ingredients."

Mrs McLeod didn't know what to say, she wasn't used to being complimented. "Och, away with you Meenister, you have the gift of the gab, I'll say that!" She was glad that Colin couldn't see her blushing. She spotted herself in the Callum's shaving mirror which hung on a nail above the kitchen sink. *"Oh mercy, look at me, am I not just the colour of a beetroot!?"* she thought.

She wondered if Colin hadn't developed a crush on her. *"Och, the poor soul, some men always want what they can't have."* She looked in the mirror again, plumped up her hair and hummed the Gaelic tune, 'Hò-rì hòró my bonny wee lass,' The Tiree Love song, as she tidied up the kitchen.

Lunch passed and Colin's nerves began to bother him at the thought that he would soon be seeing the lovely Lorna again. What would he say? What if he made a fool of himself?
What if she didn't like him?

"Are you away out this afternoon Meenister?" asked Mrs McLeod.

"Yes Mrs McLeod, did I not mention that er… Lorna is showing me around the Island today?" Colin replied.

"Oh yes, now I do remember something of the sort," Mrs McLeod smiled, she knew fine well that Colin was to meet with Lorna, but the mischief was in her.

At 1.30 pm exactly, Colin pulled up outside the Emporium and just as the wheels stopped turning, Lorna appeared, gave him a wee wave, and ran round to the passenger's side and jumped in.

Colin thought his heart would burst as he smelled her perfume, was it Lilly of the Valley or Lavender? He was no expert on perfumes but whatever it was it made his head spin.

"Hello, Colin," Lorna said sweetly.

"Hello Lorna how are you today?" he replied nervously.

Lorna giggled and said, "Oh I am just as well as I was when I saw you about an hour or so ago."

"Oh, yes, of course, how silly of me!" Colin

blushed, which prompted Lorna to touch his arm and smile.

"Ok then, where would you like to go?" she asked.

"I wonder if you would take me to see my grandmother's croft?"

"Yes of course, it's not that far from here."

Lorna gave him directions and soon they were pulling up outside a most charming little cottage. With its white walls and abundance of beautiful flowers, it really was a picture, the kind of picture you would see on the top of a box of chocolates.

"It's been quite a while since I was last over this way – it's so bonnie isn't it?" Lorna said.

"It certainly is," Colin was pleasantly surprised as many of the other crofts on the Island were in a poor state of repair.

"And it's all yours now Colin." Lorna was genuinely pleased for him.

"So it is!" he was finding it hard to take it all in.

"Well, we'd better take a look inside, where will we get the key?"

"It'll be hidden under a stone by the back door, that's where most people hide their spare key, you know, for emergencies and the like."

Sure enough, the key was 'hidden' under a stone and they let themselves in. All the curtains were closed and the mirrors covered as was the custom when someone had passed away.

As they walked in they were struck by a sweet scent. "What is that beautiful smell?" Colin asked, "Is it honeysuckle or ….."
"It's sweetpea Colin," Lorna interrupted. "I'd know it anywhere. Whenever your grandmother came into the shop that beautiful fragrance of sweetpeas filled the air. It's your grandmother Colin, she is still here and she's saying, 'Welcome home'."
Colin felt a shiver run down his spine. Although he'd never been here before, he did feel very much at home.

*'It's like going back a hundred years or more,'* Colin thought. The furniture, the curtains, the peat fire with its black range for cooking were all from another era, yet so cosy, comfortable and homely. It was as if his grandparents had been living in a

time warp, but then it could be said that much of the Western Isles were living in a time warp, but considering all that was going on in the outside world, perhaps that was no bad thing.

The pair spent an hour or so going around the house and the sheds out the back. Colin found a biscuit tin with a jumble of photographs inside. He removed the lid and a sea of faces looked out from the faded sepia pages. Some were formal and posed, while others were more relaxed as children played and adults posed in outdated clothing.

Was that his mother as a child standing in bare feet? And was that her brother Colin standing next to her?
Uncle Colin lived in Ballachulish and had been a favourite in the family. He had died quite young in an accident in the Slate Quarry, on the very same day as Colin had been born in Glasgow, and so he was named after his uncle Colin.

He decided to take the tin of photo's home with him, perhaps his aunty Bunty would be able to shed some light on the vaguely familiar faces who were looking out from the past.

As they left, making sure to 'hide' the key under the stone by the back door, Colin took a last backward look at his grandmother's croft and felt a pang of sadness to be leaving this idyllic place.

Lorna sensed his melancholy mood and laid a hand on his shoulder saying, "Don't be sad Colin, you'll be back one day."
"Yes, you're right Lorna, and thank you for bringing me here, it means a lot to me," replied Colin.
Lorna felt a warm glow inside her and thought to herself, '*He really is a lovely man, I hope and pray that he will come back one day.*'

# Chapter 16

*"Colin wasn't sure what the protocol was on kissing on the first date, having only dated one girl before…"*

◆

Once they were back in the car, they sat in silence for a few minutes, then Lorna asked, "Are you okay, Colin?"

"Yes, I'm fine thank you. I'm feeling quite emotional, it's taken me quite by surprise. I'm so glad you were here with me," he touched her hand and Lorna thought that she might faint.

They gazed at each other for a few awkward moments. Lorna would have leaned over and kissed him but didn't want to appear too forward, after all, he *was* a Minister.

Colin had the very same thought, *'Would it be too quick? Was she just being friendly and be horrified if I kissed her out of the blue?'* His expertise with the ladies was pretty much non existent so he chose to play safe and said, "Okay… well… where, in this lovely Island should we go now?"

Lorna felt a sense of disappointment but smiled

and said that there were a number of places that they could visit.

"There's Kinlochmhor Castle, the Fairy Well, the Witches Tree and the Selkies grave for a start.

How about we go over to Kinlochmhor Castle, that's not too far from here?"

"Sounds good to me," Colin said as he drove off and followed Lorna's directions.

As they were driving, Colin was admiring the beautiful scenery and he asked Lorna, "Why is the Island called Rhua? What does it mean?"

"In the Gaelic it means 'point' or a peninsular of land, and as our island is quite long but not very wide it was originally called, Eilean Rhubha by our ancestors, and that is its real name, but now we just call it Rhua. It's a very suitable name don't you think?"

"Oh yes, the Gaelic is a beautiful language and very descriptive too," Colin agreed.

"If you were staying longer. I could teach you the Gaelic," Lorna said. "I'm sure it wouldn't take you long to get the hang of it."

"I'd love that, really," he said perhaps a bit too enthusiastically, "but sadly, I have to go home tomorrow."

Colin glanced over at Lorna and saw the sadness in her face. He felt sad too.

She sensed he was looking over at her and was hoping for some token of his affection, but Colin took cold feet and started up the car and they drove on for a further few minutes in silence.

Somewhat deflated but eager to keep the conversation going, Lorna said, "It's a lovely car that you are driving Colin, is it Callum McLeod's?"

"Well, in a way, it belonged to Mrs McLeod's grandfather. Have you seen it before?" asked Colin.

"Oh yes, I work part time in the hotel and Callum comes round to the back door once or twice a week, always at night. We all admire his car."

Colin's curiosity was sparked and so he asked, "Why would Callum be coming to the hotel at night?"

"Oh, it's the fish, the chef buys them from him and puts them in the hotel freezer," replied Lorna in all innocence.

"Does he now?" Colin wasn't totally shocked.

"Turn in here!" Lorna said suddenly with a mischievous smile.

Colin had to brake quite hard to stop in time for the turning.

They drove for a few hundred yards along a gravel track and Colin stopped. He could only see a pile of stones but no castle, maybe he was missing something.

"Look, it's the castle!" Lorna said.

"Where?" Colin asked looking around.

"Over there," Lorna pointed at the pile of stones.

"Oh, right," Colin tried not to look too disappointed.

"Yes, we are very proud of our castle," Lorna said with a twinkle in her eye.

"How old is the, er … castle, Lorna?"

"Around the middle of the 13th century, we think."

"Yes, well, considering it's been around that long, it looks…well…it looks like…" Colin said.

"Like a pile of stones!" Lorna replied and they looked at each other for a second or two, and then burst out laughing.

"Yes, but what a beautiful pile of stones it is!" Colin said. They looked at each other again, which only set them off laughing once more.

After a few minutes of laughter, their eyes met and it was as if time had frozen them as they gazed at each other.

Colin felt as if his heart was going to melt away and thought he could detect Lorna slowly moving towards him – or was he slowly moving towards her?

Panic set in once more, Colin wasn't sure what the protocol was on kissing on the first date, having only dated one girl before and that wasn't really a proper date, more a case of agreeing to meet fellow student Carole in the library to study Barthian Theology – then going for a coffee.

"Oh, well, where to next?" Colin found himself saying.

Lorna looked disappointed and replied, "Oh, yes, of course," shaking herself out of her dream-like state. "Perhaps we might drive down the coast to Rob Roy's cave? It's very popular with the tourists.

"Rob Roy's cave?" Colin queried. He was pretty sure that Rob Roy never actually made it this far North, or West for that matter. He wondered if Lorna was pulling his leg again.

"Rob Roy?" he asked. "_The_ Rob Roy McGregor?"
"Oh yes, it's said that he hid in the cave to get away from the redcoats, or so the story goes. Come on, I'll show you."
"But..." Colin decided to keep silent, perhaps Rob Roy and the Redcoats really _had_ visited the remote island of Rhua.

Aye, perhaps.

# Chapter 17

*'He's very handsome, like a young Cary Grant..."*

◆

Lorna and Colin continued along the coast road in silence, but it was a comfortable and relaxed silence. *'Things are going well,'* Lorna thought to herself as she looked over at Colin who was taking in the scenery. *'He's very handsome, like a young Cary Grant,'* she thought as her mind wandered to wedding bells and a rosy future with a family and a little white cottage.

She could see that Colin was deep in thought, perhaps he was dreaming the same dreams as she was, perhaps that was why he was smiling.

But Colin, however, was wondering how many miles to the gallon this beautiful old car would do. Probably 10 to 15 miles at most, he thought, and was just about to ask Lorna how many miles *she* thought it might do, when Lorna broke the silence and asked, "Did you enjoy the Wake last night?

It took Colin a few moments to reset his mind back to the moment.

He wondered if 'enjoyed' was a suitable word for a Wake or funeral tea. In Glasgow it was referred to as 'The Purvey.'

Colin tried to be tactful, he didn't want to embarrass or upset Lorna.

"Well, yes, it was pleasant enough, but don't you think that sort of thing is a bit, well, irreverent and flippant, you know, with it being a funeral?"

"Oh no Colin, quite the opposite, it's a happy occasion! We were celebrating the life of dear Mrs McGillivray and giving her a good send off as she goes to meet her maker in Paradise."

Colin had never thought of it like that before, but he had to confess he could see her point.

"Surely going up to heaven is a glorious experience, and passing on from this life into eternal rest is something to be celebrated," Lorna said. Colin had to agree.

As he was mulling all this over, Lorna broke his train of thought by saying, "And you did well taking dram for dram with Mr McCrimmond, he fair likes a glass or two!"

"Yes, he does rather, doesn't he? I have to confess the whisky didn't seem to affect me at all!"

"Aye, maybe it was beginners luck or maybe….."

Lorna bit her tongue, had she said too much?

"Or maybe, what, Lorna?" Colin said quizzically.

"Do you not know?"

"Know what?" now Colin was *really* intrigued now.

"It was the ladies in the kitchen, they, er, they felt sorry for you and…"

"And what Lorna, what did the ladies in the kitchen do?"

"Well, every time they poured you both a dram and sent it through, they gave Mr McCrimmond a bumper dram and gave you…" she paused, "A wee drop whisky in the bottom of the glass and topped it up with Irn Bru! Did you not hear the hilarity coming from the kitchen?"

"Well, yes but I just thought……… Irn Bru?!" He shook his head.

"Yes Colin, it looks, for all the world like any other dram. They were trying to save you from a great embarrassment. Mrs Fraser said you were like 'a lamb before the wolves,' it was her idea."

"Oh Lorna, that makes things worse. They thought I was like a lamb, and here was me thinking that I had beat him fair and square." Colin went very quiet, his male ego had been severely bruised.

Lorna wished she hadn't mentioned it all, the last thing she wanted to do was upset him, with him being such a lovely man.

A few minutes later Colin said, "I could have beaten him anyway. I once drank 5 drams in one night when we were up in the Clachaig Inn at Glencoe!" *(He omitted to mention that he had been extremely ill for days afterwards.)*
"Yes, of course Colin, I am quite sure you could have."
What was one small white lie compared to a dented ego?
Colin looked over at Lorna and smiled, he knew she was just trying to be kind, and said, "Thank you," in a soft, gentle voice.

She was touched by his gentleness, and wanted to say, *"Colin I think I'm falling in love with you,"* but smiled instead and said, "That's alright Colin, you are a very special man, and everyone thinks so – including me." Lorna blushed and so did Colin.

"You're very special too Lorna," Colin said, and Lorna felt the butterflies fluttering around in her stomach. Once again. nerves got the better of Colin, and he started up the engine.

They drove in silence for a few more miles until they saw a sign painted on a dilapidated board which proclaimed ~

*The world famous Rob Roy's Cave iss here.*
*Towrists welcome.*
*Follow the path but be careful now.*
*P.S. Feel free to leave a donation in the box.*
But there was no box.

Colin couldn't help smiling as he pulled over and parked up.

He was slowly falling in love with the Islands and the people, but more especially, he was slowly falling in love with Lorna.

He would be leaving Rhua soon, weather permitting, and he wondered if he would ever see her again.

The rain was heavy by now and they sat in the car and peered out as the mist was closing in from the sea. It was getting cold, so Colin left the engine running.

After a few minutes, Lorna said, "Colin?"

"Yes, what is it?" he wondered if she was going to confess her feelings for him.

"What's that smell?" she asked.

Colin, somewhat deflated, sniffed the air, it was the smell of fish. "That old rogue Callum!" Colin said. "It's all his fishing gear in the boot, the rascal!" he said.

"It will probably be salmon on the menu at Mrs McLeod's tonight!" said Lorna, smiling. They looked at each other and burst out laughing.

They sat for what seemed like hours, talking about everything under the sun until Lorna asked, "What time is it?"

"About half past four," Colin said.

"Oh no! I'll have to be going home soon to help my mother make tea before father gets in from the shop."

"I'd better get you home then, your mum will be wondering where you are."

"Aye, she does worry about me and needs me to help around the house. She contracted Polio in her late teens and struggles to get about."

"Oh dear," Colin said, "is she badly disabled with it?"

"It affects her legs mostly. Perhaps you noticed her in the church? She was sitting at the side in a wheelchair. She thought you were great!"

"Oh yes," Colin remembered her, she was so engrossed in the service and seemed to be taking in every word. "Yes, I do remember her, she was a lovely 'smiley' lady."

"Yes, that's mum all over, never complains, always smiling."

"I'm not surprised to hear that, she seemed delightful."

After a few minutes, Colin said reluctantly, "Well, I suppose we should be going now, she'll be wondering where you are."

"Can we stay, just another 5 minutes Colin?" Lorna smiled coyly.

"How can I resist a smile as beautiful as that?" Colin's heart was racing, he had never felt like this before.

They gazed at each other and slowly moved together until their lips gently touched. They shared their first kiss and Lorna was sure her heart was about to burst. It was exactly as she dreamed it would be.

'So, <u>this</u> is how it feels to be in love,' she thought to herself and almost fainted with the emotions that were flooding through her.

"Oh Colin, I wish we could stay here forever."

"So do I, but we had better get going soon, we can't have your mum worrying, can we?"

"No, of course not, I suppose you're right." Lorna agreed, half-heartedly. She squeezed his arm and thought, '*What a lovely man, imagine him worrying about my mum.*'

# Chapter 18

*"Oh mercy, imagine me calling the Meenister by his*
*first name! Whoever would have thought…?"*

◆

Colin and Lorna drove back to Kinlochmhor in
silence, and both were ecstatically happy, but they
knew that tomorrow, their parting would be
heartbreaking.

Just before they got into the village, Lorna asked
Colin to pull in for a few minutes. She took a piece
of paper from her bag and wrote her address on it
and the telephone number of the shop.
"Here you are, my address and the telephone
number of the shop, and this is the number for the
public phone in the Hotel, if you ever want to
phone me," and she added the hotel phone
number to the note.

"Of course I'll phone you, silly. Do you have
another piece of paper? I'll give you my address
and the number of the communal phone out in the
hallway of my flat in Glasgow."

They exchanged details and hugged for a few minutes before heading on to Lorna's home.

Lorna directed Colin to pull in around the corner from the shop where the front door to the house was.

"Would you like to come in and meet my Mum? She'd love to see you," Lorna asked.

"Well er.. would that be okay? I mean, your father…?"

"Don't worry about dad, he'll do what mum tells him!" Lorna said with a smile.

"Oh well, okay then," Colin wasn't expecting this but if it meant being with Lorna for even a few minutes more, then he was happy go in and meet her mother.

Lorna's mum was in the kitchen when they went in.

"Oh, mercy me!" she said in a fluster. "It's the Meenister and here's me with my pinny on and not a brush through my hair since this morning!"

"Don't worry, Mrs MacDonald, you look bonnie just as you are. It's lovely to meet you."

Colin was the epitome of courtesy and charm.

"Lorna told me you were a lovely man, and here you are!"

"Mum!" Lorna chastised her mother for spilling her secrets.

"Lorna very kindly showed me around the Island but I'm afraid the weather was getting worse, so we had to cut our sightseeing trip short," Colin explained.

"Och, never mind, there's always tomorrow, although the weather forecast isn't so good." Lorna's mum rather liked the idea of her daughter being courted by a Minister, and him being such a lovely, well mannered young man too.

"I'm afraid I have to go back in the morning, Donald John from Coll is coming over for me at nine o'clock."

Mrs MacDonald's eyes flashed over at Lorna who was looking sad. "Don't you be worrying sweetheart, God himself will be watching over you both."

"My very words Mrs MacDonald. In God we Trust."

"Please Meenister, call me Peggy," insisted Mrs MacDonald.

"Thank you… Peggy… and please call me Colin."

"Oh mercy, imagine me calling the Meenister by his first name! Whoever would have thought?"

"Will you be staying for your tea, Meenis…. sorry,… Colin?"

"Thank you but sadly no… Peggy… Mrs McLeod has dinner waiting for me at the croft, it would be impolite if I were to let her down. Perhaps another time?"

"Of course, Colin, you are welcome here whenever you like," Peggy offered.

Lorna was pleased that her mother and Colin were getting on. *'It bodes well for the future,'* she thought, whatever the future might bring.

"Well, I had better be going, I wouldn't like to incur the wrath of Mrs McLeod," Colin said.

"Oh mercy, no," said Peggy MacDonald in a serious tone. "You don't want to be doing that!" prompting Colin to head for the door.

"Goodbye then Mrs MacDon….Peggy, it's been a pleasure meeting you and I do hope we shall meet again."

"So do I Colin, don't be a stranger," said Lorna's mother with a deep, warm smile.

Lorna followed Colin to the front door and they both had tears in their eyes. Lorna said, "We *will* meet again, won't we Colin?"

"Yes, we will my darling I promise you that. I don't know how or when but we *will* be together again, I promise."

They hugged each other as tightly as they could and let the tears flow.

Colin tried to pull away gently but Lorna clung on and wouldn't let him go.

"Please don't go, say you'll stay!" she sobbed.

"But I *must* go Lorna, I really must."

"I know, but I am so frightened that I won't see you ever again!" and she held Colin even closer.

After a few more minutes Lorna stood back and calmed herself.

Reluctantly Colin got into his car as Lorna blew a kiss to him and ran indoors in floods of tears.

Colin sat in the car for a few moments as he composed himself. It had been an unexpected whirlwind and it was as if it had all been a wonderful, breathtaking dream.

He was about to pull away when the house door opened and Lorna ran out and tapped on the car window.

"Mum's just told me that dad is going to be closing the shop tomorrow morning for a couple of hours for stock taking, but he's going to leave the door open between nine o'clock to ten for 'emergencies.' *I* think he just doesn't want to miss the chance of a sale!

I don't suppose you could pop in to see me at the shop before you go?"

"Oh, I wish I could sweetheart but Donald John is picking me up at the jetty at nine o'clock in the morning."

"Oh yes, of course... I was just thinking..." and she started to cry again.

"Well, there is one thing I want to say before you go – I love you Colin Campbell!" and she put her head inside the car and they kissed their last kiss, for now, anyway.

"I love you too, Lorna MacDonald!"

Reluctantly Lorna stood back, crying sad yet happy tears too.

Colin drove off, his heart was beating double fast. He looked in the rear view mirror, Lorna was waving. He waved back and then turned the corner and drove over the hill to Mrs McLeod's wee croft.

# Chapter 19

*"The 'Conversation is a great thing…"*

◆

Colin pulled into the ramshackle garage at the side of Mrs McLeod's croft and sat for a few minutes to compose himself.

The past couple of days had been a whirlwind. Who could have imagined that just a few days ago he was sitting in his study in Kelvinside with his cat Moses on his knee wondering where on earth the island of Rhua was?

A lot had happened in those few days – and now he was going back to Glasgow, leaving this beautiful Island and its delightful people. But more importantly, he was leaving the lovely Lorna MacDonald behind and he knew he would miss her terribly.

He was feeling quite emotional when he heard Mrs McLeod shouting, "Is it yourself Meenister? Your tea is almost ready."

"Just coming Mrs McLeod." He wondered if Mrs McLeod knew about Lorna and himself. She certainly seemed to know everything else that was going on in the Island without ever leaving her croft.

He checked his face in the rear view mirror, his eyes were still quite red, perhaps Mrs McLeod wouldn't notice.

*'Who am I kidding?'* he thought, *'she'll notice the second I walk through the door!'*

"Good evening Meenister," Mrs McLeod said as Colin walked into the kitchen. "How did your afternoon of touring go with Lorna, did you see the sights of Rhua?"

"Oh yes, it went very well thank you, except for the weather," Colin said casually.

"Aye, it's not weather for getting out of the car. Did you enjoy Rob Roy's cave?"

*'How on earth did she know?'* Colin thought, and without thinking said, "How did you know we were sitting there, Mrs McLeod? We were just chatting to see if the rain would go off."

"Oh, Mrs Chisholm passed by on her bike and saw you there and said you make such a lovely couple."

"We're not 'a couple,' Mrs McLeod we were just passing the time as the rain was on." Colin feared that the 'jungle drums' had been sending messages around the island already.

"Of course, Meenister, of course, did I not say the very same thing to Mrs Chisholm myself?" she said with a knowing smile.

"Thank you Mrs McLeod, I appreciate that, how long will tea be?"

"Oh, about 10 minutes or so."

"That's grand, I'll go to my room and read a passage or two from the Scriptures."

"Ah yes, the Holy Book, just the very thing for lifting the spirits, with all that good news and everything," Mrs McLeod said as she studied Colin's face for some sign of response.

*'She knows,'* he thought to himself, *'She knows!'*

Colin went through to his room, sat on the bed and suddenly felt very emotional. The tears were beginning to well up when there was a knock on his bedroom.

Mrs McLeod spoke through the door, "I forgot to say, a note came from the Post Office with a message from Donald John."

"Oh, do come in Mrs McLeod," Colin said as he quickly wiped his eyes.

"Here you are Meenister, my apologies," and she handed the note to him. "Dear me, are you feeling alright? I noticed whenever you came in that your eyes were very red."

"Oh, it's alright Mrs McLeod, just a touch of Hay-fever, I think."

"Aye, that will be it," Mrs McLeod answered with more than a hint of suspicion. She left the room and Colin read his note from Donald John.

The note said, *"Poor weather forecast for the morning. To be better later – will pick you up at the jetty on the one o'clock tide. More time with Lorna! Stop."*

'Great news!' but how on earth did he know about Lorna, *he had only met her the night before? 'Probably a passing seagull!'* Colin thought and smiled.

"Tea is ready Meenister," called Mrs McLeod.

"Coming," Colin called back. "What do we have tonight, Mrs McLeod?" Colin asked eagerly.

"Two lovely fresh poached eggs, from our very own hen and toasted soda bread made with my very own hands," Mrs McLeod said proudly. "And I have made an apple pie with fruit from Mrs Chisholm's apple tree, she popped round with them this afternoon, and her on her bike too."

"Gosh, you really are spoiling me, with poached salmon for lunch and now poached eggs for tea. Which reminds me, I haven't had the pleasure of meeting Mr McLeod yet."

All this talk of poaching reminded him of Callum, Mrs McLeod's husband.

He realised what he had just said as he glanced over at Mrs McLeod who seemed to be rising above it.

"I meant… I mean, how nice it would be to meet your husband before I leave tomorrow and by the way, Donald John will now be picking me up at one o'clock tomorrow afternoon."

"It's the Lord's hand that is in it – doesn't the good book tell us that the Lord works in mysterious ways?" said Mrs McLeod.

Colin had to agree. He never ceased to be amazed at Gods' helping hand, just when it was most needed.

"Mr McLeod should be home shortly. He is working later tonight. Will you be needing the car? It's just that he uses it for work, and he takes it for a run round the Island at night when the traffic is not so heavy," Mrs McLeod said in all seriousness.

Colin looked up at Mrs McLeod, thinking that she was joking. *'After all,'* he thought, *'was the traffic <u>ever</u> heavy on Rhua?'*

Mrs McLeod was not known for her sense of humour and she carried on washing the pots and pans, completely unaware of Colin's wry smile.

A few minutes passed and Colin heard the back door being opened.
"Oh, it's himself!" said Mrs McLeod.
"Callum, come away through and say hello to the Meenister."

In walked a rotund, red faced man with a big smile. So *this* was the infamous Callum McLeod!

"Hello Meenister, we meet at last, how are you?"
"I am well, thank you Mr McLeod."
"Och, call me Callum. Is my good lady looking after you well?"
"Oh yes, Mrs McLeod is being exceptionally kind."
"Och, away with you!" said Mrs McLeod with an embarrassed smile.
"Oh yes, she has the good name far and wide as the best Bed and Breakfast establishment in all of Rhua!" Callum said with great pride.
"And rightly so!" agreed Colin, being too much of a gentleman to mention that he knew she was the *only* B&B on Rhua.

Mrs McLeod blushed with embarrassment - *but she was secretly enjoying the adulation.*

"Will you be wanting the car tonight Meenister? It's just that I have a bit of.. er.. business to attend to?" asked Callum.

"No, no, I won't be needing it, thank you. And what is it you do Callum?" Colin had the devil in him.

After a few moments of awkward silence, Callum said, "Oh, it's the 'Conversation', it keeps me very busy, especially at nights," he explained.

Colin wondered if he meant, *'Conservation'* and said, "Oh, Conservation is it Callum? That's good work."
Callum was a little bemused and looked to Mrs McLeod.
"That's right Meenister," she said. "It's the 'Conservation' that he is involved with, isn't it Callum?"
Callum finally twigged and said, "Oh, yes, I save the fish from those terrible poachers – and from the otters too, vicious wee brutes. Aye, the Conversation is a great thing."
"Yes indeed," replied Colin with a smile.

Callum and Mrs McLeod looked at each other and smiled, quite sure that they had very cleverly pulled the wool over the Meenister's eyes.

Colin smiled and tucked into his tea.

"Delicious eggs Mrs McLeod," said Colin. "Poached, just as I like them."

# Chapter 20

*"...he's a good man even although he sometimes drives me to Timbuck Two and back!..."*

◆

The next morning Colin was up early and had packed his case by 8am.

"My, it's early that you are this morning, Meenister," said Mrs McLeod, "Will you be going into the village?" Mrs McLeod had guessed that he would be going in to see Lorna before he left the Island.

"Er… yes, I thought I might pop in for a final look around now that Donald John isn't coming for me until one o'clock," Colin replied, knowing full well that Mrs McLeod had rumbled him.

"Aye, just that," said Mrs McLeod with a knowing smile.

"Your breakfast will be a wee while yet, I'm afraid Meenister. Callum is not long in from his work and he has brought in two lovely sea trout for your breakfast, I'll fry them for you, with oatmeal."

"That sounds lovely Mrs McLeod, there's no

hurry," Colin said. "Where is Callum? I was hoping to say goodbye to him before I left."

"He has gone to his bed for an hour or two. Oh, the hours that man puts in for the Conservatorial Society, some nights he's out all night. It'll be the death of him!"

"Oh my goodness, don't be saying that Mrs McLeod, heaven forbid!"

"It's only the wishful thinking Meenister, I wouldn't change him for all the tea in China, or is it, India? Oh well, either way, he's a good man even although he sometimes drives me to Timbuck Two and back!"

"Yes, Love is patient, love is kind, as the Bible tells us, Mrs McLeod."

"Oh mercy, I wouldn't go so far as to say *that*, Meenister!"

Colin wasn't quite sure how to respond so he smiled and said, "I'll just pop out and open the garage door and get the car ready before it rains, I won't be long."

"Yes, you do that and I'll get the breakfast on."

Colin gently opened the garage door for fear it might fall off again and was immediately struck by the heavy aroma of fish. *'Callum was busy last night, the rogue!'* he thought to himself with a smile.

He reversed the car outside and opened the boot and all the windows and doors. *'That should clear the air a bit,'* he thought as he walked back into the croft.

Mrs McLeod was just covering the fish with oatmeal and placing them into the frying pan as Colin walked into the kitchen.

"Just a few minutes until breakfast," she said.

"Excellent," Colin replied, "I have some scriptures to read, so I'll go through to the bedroom and will be back shortly."

"Aye, just that," came the reply.

Colin went through and took a small Bible from his coat pocket. He liked to gain some comfort and assurance from Scripture before setting off on a journey.

He began to read from the book of Psalms at Psalm 121, "*I lift up mine eyes unto to the hills, from whence doth come mine aid...*"

Then Colin turned to the New Testament, at the

Gospel of Luke Chapter 4 and verse 10 and read, *"The Lord will command his Angels concerning you, to watch over you carefully."*

Duly comforted, he smiled contentedly, said a prayer, put his Bible away and went through for breakfast.

After breakfast he drove into the village. He was looking forward to surprising Lorna and seeing her once more.

He was a bit early and he knew that the Emporium wouldn't be open yet so he went round to the door of the house and knocked, hoping that Lorna would open it but it was Lorna's mother in her wheelchair who came to the door.

"Oh mercy me! It is yourself!" she said with a large smile on her face. "It will be Lorna that you are looking for."

"Yes, Mrs MacDonald is she in? I thought I'd surprise her."

"She is with her father in the shop early today Meenister. They have been so busy these past few weeks that they are having to do a stock-take while it is quiet, and they have a big order coming in off the ferry next week. Just you go round and knock on the shop door. Oh, she will be so excited to be seeing you!"

"Thank you Mrs MacDonald, it's lovely to see you again."

"Now, Colin, it's Peggy, remember, not Mrs MacDonald!" she smiled.

"Oh yes, of course, Peggy. Every Blessing to you."

He walked round and knocked on the shop door. "Sorry, we're not open yet," a soft voice replied. It was Lorna's voice.

Colin mischievously knocked again.

"We're not open yet!" the voice was louder this time.

Colin knocked a third time. "Alright, wait now," said Lorna.

He heard the door being unlocked and as Lorna opened the door, she saw it was Colin. "Oh my goodness, it's yourself!" and she flung her arms around his neck and started to cry. "I thought I might never see you again, but here you are!" and she hugged Colin even tighter.

"Donald John isn't picking me up until one o'clock now and I couldn't go without seeing you before I left."

As they stood at the shop doorway hugging each other, oblivious to the world, two of the local ladies, Isabel Chisholm and Betty McLeod walked by and seeing the door open, tried to get into the shop.

"Tut tut," said Betty, "Is it not terrible when good, God fearing folks can't get by for young people kissing each other in shop doorways!"

"Aye Betty, the young ones today! Would never have happened in our day!" said her friend Isabel and they made a great show of struggling to get past and into the shop.

"Oh goodness, I am sorry ladies," said a flustered Lorna as she broke away from Colin and pulled at her frock and straightened her hair.

"And him a Meenister too, shameful!" said Isabel as they went into the shop.

Colin and Lorna looked at each other and both stifled a laugh.

"You had better come inside sweetheart, that's the rain on," Lorna said taking his arm.

"I thought you were supposed to be leaving at nine o'clock, what happened, did Donald John sleep in after a late night 'fishing?' Lorna asked with a smile.

"No, he is picking me up at one o'clock now, so I just had to come and see you before I left."

"Oh Colin, it's a wonderful surprise!" and Lorna hugged him again.

Her father saw it was Colin and said in a loud voice, "Mercy me, if it isn't yourself, Meenister!" and he gave him a good, firm handshake. "Please, call me Colin, Mr MacDonald."

"Oh that is kind of you Meenist...or should I say, Colin."

The more he thought about it, the more he liked the idea of having a Minister for a son-in-law, *'better than the wasters who hang around the village,'* he thought to himself. Not only that, having a Minister in the family wouldn't do his reputation as a shop owner and local businessman any harm either. Win, win.

Mr MacDonald looked over at the two ladies who had just come into the shop, "Hello ladies, I'm afraid the Emporium isn't open just yet, we are taking note of the stock, what with us being so busy."

Mr MacDonald was never known to turn a customer away, so he said, "But now that you are here, I wouldn't want to disappoint you, so if there is anything you see that interests you, I am happy to oblige you. We have a new range of coloured hair nets, the latest thing from Oban."

"Coloured hair nets? Whatever next!" said Mrs Chisholm. "Well, now that we are here it wouldn't do any harm to have a wee look would it, Mr MacDonald?"

"Absolutely not Mrs Chisholm, they're over there beside the new Nylons, we haven't had a chance to lay them out yet, what with us being so busy." Mr McDonald never missed a chance to let people know how well he is doing.

He knew that Isabel Chisholm and Betty McLeod would 'pass on' anything of interest to the rest of the village and it would do no harm to mention just how busy the shop was.

The two ladies feigned an interest in the coloured hair nets and were straining their ears to catch every word between Lorna and 'the Meenister.'

When they saw that Colin and Lorna had stopped talking, Betty said loudly, "Oh look at the colours Isabel – there's yellow, purple, red and blue - and here's a green one! My, my, what will they think of next?"

"Whatever was wrong with the brown ones?" Isabel replied.

Both of the ladies shook their heads in despair at the new fangled fashions of the day. "Brown was good enough for my mother and it's good enough for me, mind you, this red one *is* rather racy isn't it?" said Betty holding it up.

"Aye Betty, it would fair set the tongues wagging!"

"I suppose you are right Isabel, the gossips would be calling me the 'scarlet woman,' to be sure!"

And they both giggled at the thought of it.

# Chapter 21

*"Mrs Chisholm! Would you be so kind as to stop interfering with the gentleman's combinations!"*

◆

Mr MacDonald didn't want the ladies to overhear the conversations with the Minister, which was exactly what the ladies were hoping for, so he said, "Come away through," and he led Colin and Lorna through to the back of the shop and into his small office. "We don't want the whole world to hear our conversations, do we?"

"Indeed no, Mr MacDonald."

Colin smiled, thinking that two ladies in a small shop, on a remote Scottish island, hardly constituted 'the whole world.'

"I have just spoken to your good lady and she is looking well," Colin said.

"Och, she is an angel to be sure Meenister, she suffers but never complains, does she not, Lorna?"

"That's right father, mother is an example to us all."

"Aye, just as you say, just as you say. And what brings you into our world famous Emporium today, Meenister? As if I didn't know, eh Lorna, eh?"

Lorna blushed, "Father! Don't be embarrassing the Meenister, he just kindly popped in to say goodbye to us before he leaves for the mainland."

"Yes, Mr MacDonald, I thought I would come to wish you well and take one last look at your amazing 'world famous' Emporium before Donald John comes to pick me up." Colin had his fingers crossed behind his back as he spoke. Lorna saw Colin's crossed fingers and smiled.

Mr MacDonald beamed with pride, "Yes, we are very proud of our humble establishment aren't we Lorna?" and he gave a slight bow at the word 'humble.'

"Yes father," agreed Lorna, "Very proud."

Colin got the impression that Lorna didn't have quite the same enthusiasm for the 'Emporium' as her father.

Meanwhile, the two ladies were pretending to browse the various items as they stealthily made their way down to the office so they could better hear what was being said.

"I was wondering if Lorna might be able to help me choose a small gift for Mrs MacLeod? She has been so kind to me during my stay here," Colin asked.

"Of course, Meenist… er Colin. Away Lorna and help Colin to find something suitable. We have some new sheets fresh in from Oban, made from the purest flannelette. Or there are those new black Nylons, the sheer ones – no, no, perhaps not for Mrs MacLeod."

"We'll find something, don't worry father. Come on Colin let's look over here." Lorna led Colin over to a large wooden table with a selection of towels, sheets and the like.

"I'm sorry about father," Lorna said. "He has the grand ideas about his Emporium, I'm sure he thinks that the visitors believe it's the Rhua branch of the famous shop in London!"

As Mr MacDonald walked out of the office, he noticed the two ladies standing quite close to the office door. Their heads were down, hoping they wouldn't be noticed.

He knew exactly what they were up to. "Ladies! What are you doing in this section of the Emporium? These items are for the gentlemen." He noticed that Isabel was holding a pair of men's 'long Johns' in her hand. "Mrs Chisholm! Would you be so kind as to stop interfering with the gentleman's combinations!"

Mrs Chisholm immediately dropped the 'offending item,' not realising that she had it in her hand as she had been too engrossed in eavesdropping at the office door.

"Oh my goodness, whatever must you think?" Isabel said in her own defence. "I'm not in the way of handling gentlemen's under garments, I can assure you of that! The very thought!"

Mr MacDonald was having none of it.

"It's a terrible thing when men's unmentionables is not safe from being interfered with! I'll have to ask you ladies to leave the premises, just for today"

*"What is the world coming to when women go about handling gentlemen's unmentionables in public!"* Mr

MacDonald mumbled to himself.

The ladies were mortified at being caught eavesdropping. Mrs Chisholm sniffed and said, "Come on Betty, it is time for the Guild committee meeting anyway."
Lorna and Colin were keeping their heads down and trying not to laugh out loud.

"How about these?" Lora giggled as she picked up a pair of black, 'Midnight Rendezvous' sheer nylon stockings, "Straight from Paris, it says on the packet."
"Oh dear me no," Colin laughed. "I can't see Mrs MacLeod wearing those!"
"I should hope not!" reprimanded Lorna with another giggle.

"Now this is more like it." Lorna held up a fluffy white Tea Cosy in the shape of a West Highland Terrier's head. There was a hole for the spout at its little black nose and another for the handle on its back, by its wee tail."
"What about this, Colin?" Lorna said as she held it up.

"Oh, that's cute, what is it? " Colin asked.

"It's a tea cosy silly, it's ideal for Mrs McLeod, she likes a Strupag."

"What's a strupag?" asked Colin.

"It's what you might call in Glasgow *a wee cup of tea and a biscuit or a scone.*"

"Perfect, she'll love that. I'll take another one, one for my housekeeper, Mrs McRae, back in Glasgow."

Lorna smiled and took the gifts over to the till whereupon her father made a bee line across the shop and proceeded to wrap the tea cosies in white tissue paper.

"An excellent choice Meenister, and I'll wrap them in the very best tissue paper that Oban has to offer," he said.

"That is very kind Mr MacDonald, how much do I owe you?"

"Och no, it's on the house!" he said loudly, looking around at the other shoppers who had wandered in. "Yes, on the house. Think of it as a gift from Harrold's World Famous Emporium. Tell all your friends," and he swept his arms around in a great gesture, reminding everyone of just what a good and generous man he is.

"Thank you very much Mr MacDonald," said Colin. Mr MacDonald bowed, shaking his head in humble recognition of such unwarranted praise.

Colin whispered in Lorna's ear, "Can you get away for a wee while?"

Lorna winked and turned to her father saying, "Father, can you spare me from the shop for an hour or two?" with appealing eyes.

"Of course, sweetheart, we can stay on a bit tonight to finish the stock-take, off you go now." Her father was only too pleased to encourage the relationship between his daughter and the Minister – it was good for Lorna and good for his business too.

It was 9.30am when Lorna and Colin jumped into the car and drove off excitedly, they had a few hours or so before Colin would have to make his way to the jetty to meet Donald John.

They both knew where they would go, the place where they had first kissed, at the 'world famous'

Rob Roy's Cave.

The clouds were gathering and just as they drove into the car park the rain began to fall.  It reminded them of their last visit there when the rain was so heavy they couldn't get out of the car for fear of getting soaked.

But today, their precious time was for talking and making plans.

# Chapter 22

*"A Minister with a motorbike!*
*Lorna was impressed..."*

◆

They sat looking out at the mist coming down and the rain getting heavier. The white horses on the sea were blowing up whiter by the minute.

Lorna realised that Colin had gone quiet.

"You're very quiet Colin, are you alright?"

"Just thinking…"

"Just thinking about what?"

Colin remained silent, not sure if he should share his thoughts. Was it too soon?

"Well, I was wondering,.." he was lost for words.

"Were you wondering if we would ever see each other again?"

Colin looked over at Lorna in surprise. "Yes, but how did…?"

"Because I was thinking the very same thing," Lorna said almost in tears. "I couldn't bear it if…."

"Neither could I," replied Colin.

They held each other tightly and neither of them ever wanted to let go.

"Do you *have* to go back to Glasgow? Can't you stay just a wee bit longer? Please say you can." Her tears began to flow down her cheeks.

Colin felt the same as they sat in melancholy silence.

"Yes, I'm afraid I *have* to go back Lorna."

"But… but…" Lorna sobbed and laid her head on his shoulder.

"We *will* see each other again, I'm sure of that!" Colin said confidently.

"But when Colin, when?"

"That is in God's hands Lorna, we must put our trust in Him, He will find a way, I am certain of that, don't worry yourself. God is always faithful to those who are faithful to him," Colin assured Lorna.

"Oh I do hope so, darling, I do hope so," Lorna sobbed and squeezed Colin even tighter.

They promised that whatever happened, they *would* see each other again, but deep in their hearts, they both feared that circumstances might prevent that from happening.

"Oh, I do so wish you could stay Colin, I'm going to miss you *so* much," Lorna sniffled as she spoke. "Or I could come with you to Glasgow." Lorna knew that wasn't going to happen, but she was grasping at straws.

Colin promised that he would come back to Rhua to see her before too long.
Lorna promised that if they could get someone to look after her mother, then she would come down to Glasgow for a visit.

They both felt better that at least a provisional plan was made, and they stayed there in each other's arms, not speaking, for what seemed like an age.

Lorna broke the silence and asked, "Colin, can I ask you something?"
"Yes of course, what is it?"
She was hesitant to ask as she feared what his answer might be. She took a deep breath and said, "Is there someone at home waiting for you?"
"Yes Lorna, I'm afraid there is…."
Lorna's face dropped.

"My cat, Moses!"

"Och, you!" and she smacked his arm playfully and laid her head on his shoulder.

"But we hardly know each other Colin, how can we feel this way so soon?"

"You're right, but there are some things you just know in your heart."

They were both convinced that they had found their soul-mate and were determined not to let go.

Colin broke the silence saying, "Perhaps we should know a bit more about each other, our interests and so on."

"Good idea Colin, you go first," Lorna replied.

"Oh, right, well, where do I start? Em.... well, I was born in Glasgow, I'm 26 years old, graduated from Glasgow University with a Bachelor of Arts and a Divinity Degree. I like hillwalking, mostly in Glencoe, and I have a motorbike."

"A motorbike? Good for you!" A Minister with a motorbike! Lorna was impressed.

"Wow! I can't match all that! Do you have a church in Glasgow?" Lorna asked.

"Yes and no," Colin explained that he was working as an Assistant in a big church but was looking for a church of his own.

"Do you have any plans?" Lorna asked.

"Well, I thought I had, but now I'm not so sure." Lorna's face brightened up again.

"But what about you Lorna?"

"Well, I was born on Coll and when I was 10 my mum and dad moved over to Rhua to take over the shop. I'm 23 now and I'll be 24 next month. When I was 12, I was supposed to go over to Oban and stay in the Hostel and go to the High school but my mum didn't want me to go so far away and only come home 3 or 4 times in the year like the other children on the island, so she got permission from the school board to home-school me herself, seeing as she had been a teacher on Foula some years before. I loved being at home all year round, seeing all the different seasons."

"And what did you want to do when you left the school?"

"I've always wanted to be a teacher, working with the wee ones but I don't suppose I ever will be, it's just a dream."

"Never give up on your dream Lorna, you'd make a brilliant teacher, the children would love you!"

"Aww, thank you Colin, but living away out here, I don't think I will get the chance to go to college or whatever is needed, but I help Mrs McCrimmond with the Sunday School."

"You don't need qualifications to prove that you can communicate with children Lorna, I'd say that you were a natural!"

"Och, you're so kind, caring and positive Colin, and you are a great Meenister too!"

"Well... em..." Colin wasn't used to getting such praise. "I just have to be myself I suppose, it's all I can do."

"I'm sorry if I embarrassed you Colin but you really *are* very special, everyone says so, especially me – but then, I'm biased!"

Colin smiled.

"What kind of church are you looking for?"

"I don't know Lorna, but one thing is for sure, I want to make a difference to people's lives, you know, helping others, especially those in need," Colin said sincerely. "I would probably be happier in the poorer areas of Glasgow where the need is greatest."

"Oh, but there is a great need up here in the Islands too, you know."
"In the Islands?" Colin looked surprised, "but life here is so idyllic."
"Yes, on the surface, but we have problems too, with loneliness, the drinking, marriage breakups and more, you would be surprised Colin.
We may have our funny ways, but we have good hearts and there is a great need for a Minister who cares for the people."

"Well, I never would have thought that," Colin said wondering where the conversation was going.
"Oh yes, people think we are so happy away out here, and mostly we are, but it has its problems too."
"Well, that's certainly food for thought," Colin said pensively.

"It certainly is!" Lorna smiled as their eyes met and they both felt that the seeds of a plan were beginning to fall into place.

Colin looked at his watch and was surprised how the time had flown. "I'll have to make tracks soon sweetheart, Donald John will here soon and I have to go in by Mrs McLeod's to pick up my bag."

"Oh, do you *have* to go?" Lorna pouted.
"Yes sweetpea, I really must," and as Colin tried to break away from Lorna's arms, Lorna held on even tighter.

"I'm never going to let you go!" she said and the two tussled playfully until Colin managed to free himself and turn on the car ignition.

They drove over to the McLeod croft and as they entered the kitchen, they were greeted by Callum and Mrs McLeod.
"Oh mercy, it's young Lorna MacDonald!" Callum said with a smile. "My goodness, I swear you get bonnier every time I see you!" Lorna blushed.

"Don't be embarrassing the poor girl, you old charmer," said Mrs McLeod, thinking that she couldn't remember the last time he had given her such a compliment.

"I'm just in to pick up my case and say 'thank you' for looking after me so well Mrs MacLeod, oh, and to give you this," and he handed her the gift from the Emporium.

"Och Meenister, you shouldn't have bothered about me, I'm only too happy to give you lodgings – and you a man of God."

"Well, it was very kind of you," said Colin, "and very much appreciated. If I should find myself back on Rhua would you honour me by allowing me stay in your lovely home once again?"

Colin had made two good friends in Mr and Mrs MacLeod and was told in no uncertain terms that if ever he came back to Rhua he was to stay with no-one else, there would always be a bed for him in the McLeod croft.

"Will you take a wee Strùpag with us before you go, Meenister?" Mr McLeod asked.

Lorna looked at Colin, "Do we have time?"

"Och yes, we have more than half an hour yet and it's only a five minute walk to the jetty," Colin said looking at this watch.

"Grand! you can taste some of Mrs McLeod's famous gooseberry jam," said Callum with a beaming smile which lit up his cheery face.

Colin was anxious to show that he knew some of the Gaelic. He looked at Lorna, cleared his throat and said to the McLeod's, "Oh yes, a strupag, a wee cup of tea, moran taing. That would be grand."

Callum laughed loudly and slapped his knee saying, "Aye, you'll do Meenister. You'll do!"

"Good for you Meenister!" said Mrs McLeod "Now you can talk to the good Lord in His own tongue!"

The tea was poured and the scones were served warm, straight from the oven. Mrs McLeod's homemade gooseberry jam with thick warm cream completed the simple yet sumptuous 'strupag.'

Colin thought to himself, *'Surely this must be what it's like in Heaven,'* and he looked at Lorna and realised that Angels really *do* exist on earth.

# Chapter 23

*"Come away in lassie and sit yourself down,*
*I'll make us all a nice cup of tea..."*

◆

They chatted for a while until Colin saw the time on the clock on the mantelpiece.

"Time to be going I'm afraid," he said. "Donald John will be here soon, I'd better not keep him waiting or we'll miss the tide."

"So soon? The pier is only a short walk, can you not stay a wee while longer?" said Callum. Lorna's stomach took a lurch at the thought of him leaving.

"Well, maybe another 5 minutes and then I really will have to go," said Colin with a sad look on his face.

After a few minutes Colin went through to the bedroom and picked up his small case and hat and threw his coat over his arm.

"Well, that's me," he said. "Will you walk me down to the jetty, Lorna?"

"Of course, sweetheart," Lorna rose and they made for the door.

"Goodbye folks," Colin said to Mr and Mrs McLeod, "It's been a pleasure meeting you both and I mean that most sincerely."

Mrs McLeod had a tear in her eye and took a small embroidered handkerchief from the sleeve of her cardigan and dabbed her eyes.

"The pleasure has been all ours Meenister. May the good Lord watch over you, and be sure to come back to visit us soon."

"Yes, I'll be back, you can be sure of that."

Lorna smiled, then tears began to flow down her cheeks.

"Och, I promised myself I wouldn't cry!" Lorna was annoyed with herself.

"Never you mind," said Mrs McLeod, "Cry all you like, it's a good man that you have and he's worth every tear." And she went over and put her arms around Lorna.

All four of them had a tear in their eye and a lump in their throat.

"Take care and may God bless you both," Colin said, and he and Lorna left the croft.

Callum called out, "Now, Lorna, drop in here on your way back and I'll give you a lift back to the village, I have some 'business to attend to at the hotel," he smiled and winked.

"I will, and thank you Mr McLeod," Lorna replied, not sure whether to smile or cry – she and Colin both knew exactly what Callum's 'business at the hotel' would be about.

They walked hand in hand down to the jetty in silence. Lorna couldn't hold back the tears and Colin put his arm around her as they walked the last few yards.

Colin spotted a wee boat in the distance heading toward the Island. "There's Donald John," he said, which caused Lorna to give a sob, and they hugged even tighter.

"We _will_ see each other again won't we?" Lorna asked, looking for reassurance.

"Of course we will sweetpea, I promise. I have to come back before too long to sort out my grandmother's croft," replied Colin and he kissed her on the forehead, he was struggling to hold back the tears too.

Donald John tied up his small boat and walked up to Colin and Lorna.

"Ah it is yourself Meenister! And Lorna too, how are you? Is your mother keeping well?"

Lorna looked up but couldn't find the strength to reply, so she just gave a weak smile and a nod.

"Oh dear, Lorna," said Donald John. "Where's that bonnie smile?"

At that, Lorna burst into tears and tried to apologise through her sobbing.

"My, but it's some effect that you have on the ladies, Meenister!"

"Aye, Donald John, it's a sad day, but as I said to Lorna, we'll meet again."

"Just like thon Vera Lynn song!" Donald John joked.

Any other time it might have brought a smile, but today Colin and Lorna weren't in the mood for jokes.

"I'll have to go sweetheart," Colin said, "and you should get back to the shop to help your father, don't wait here, the rain isn't far away."

"I don't care if I get wet! My father can wait on me for once. I'm going to see you off!" Lorna said firmly.

Colin could see that Lorna meant what she said and so gave her a hug and said, "Okay sweetheart, just as you say yourself," and he realized just how much of the Highland lilt he had picked up in his voice.

Donald John noticed it too. "Aye, we'll make a highland gentleman of you yet Meenister, but for now we must go with the tide," and he picked up Colin's coat and small case and walked down to the boat. He started up the engine and waited while the two love birds said their goodbyes.

Colin walked down the jetty and Lorna stood with tears running down her cheeks.

After a short distance, Colin stopped, turned around and said loudly, "Lorna, "Tha gaol agam ort!" *(ha gail akam orsht – I love you)* in his best Gaelic tongue. Lorna burst into tears and ran down and into Colin's waiting arms. "Oh Colin, I love you too!" and they hugged for a few more minutes until Donald John shouted, "Come on young Lochinvaar, we have to go!"

Colin reluctantly tore himself away from Lorna and boarded the boat.

Donald John opened the throttle and the small boat moved away from the shore as Colin and Lorna waved to each other until the boat was just a dot in the distance.

Lorna walked back to the McLeod's croft, sobbing as she went.

Mrs McLeod gave her a hug and said, "Come away in lassie and sit yourself down, I'll make us all a nice cup of tea and then Callum will run you home."

# Chapter 24

*"Come away up to the croft Meenister,*
*there is a wee dram waiting for you..."*

◆

Colin spent much of the sea journey to Coll in silence, and Donald John respected his need for peace and quiet.

After some time, Donald John said, "Aye, she's a bonnie lass right enough is Lorna, I knew her family well. Her grandfather was a good Coll man, we would often go fishing together." Colin smiled as he knew exactly what Donald John meant by, 'fishing.' Poaching was in their genes.

"Aye," Colin replied in good Highland fashion, bringing a smile to Donald John's face.

*'The Meenister is fairly smitten,'* Donald John thought to himself. *'I'll not be surprised if he's back with us before long.'*

But Colin's mind was full of 'what if's?'
*'What if I don't get back up here?'*
*'What if Lorna finds someone else?'*
*'What if ....'*

Donald John sensed that Colin was uneasy and said, "Don't you be worrying Meenister, the good Lord is watching over you both, put your trust in Him."

Did Donald John have the 'gift' and know what he was thinking? Colin would not have been surprised if he had. It was not uncommon for Highland and Island folk to retain 'gifts' that the more sophisticated societies have long since lost. Living so close to Nature with all its wonders and mysteries, gives a sensitivity and receptiveness to such things.

Colin felt a wave of calm come over him.

"Of course, you are right Donald John. How silly of me, why am I worrying? I must hand it over to God who will do His own will, whatever that might be. Thank you, my good friend, you are a wise man indeed."

"A wise man you say? Well, I've been called many things but never have I been called 'wise'!" and he gave a loud laugh which was so infectious that Colin laughed too.

After a few minutes, Donald John said how impressed he was with Colin's Gaelic farewell to

Lorna. "Where did you learn the Gaelic Meenister? It's a dark horse that you are!"

"Callum MacLeod gave me lessons," replied Colin.

"That old rogue! It's a wonder he didn't teach you the sweary words!" They both laughed out loud again.

Two friends enjoying a laugh together, it was enough to give Colin a warm glow in his stomach and he knew that somehow, everything was going to be alright.

"Land ahoy!" shouted Donald John and pointed over Colin's shoulder. Coll was in sight.

Colin was looking forward to meeting Donald John's lovely family once again.

As they came near the shore, Donald John cut the engine and Colin saw a small group of people waiting to greet them.

Drawing closer, he could see that it was Rhona, Donald John's wife and their two daughters, Mhàiri and Kirsty.

The girls were excited and waded in up to their knees to pull the boat the final few feet up onto the white sandy beach.

"Where have you been Donald John? I was getting worried," called Rhona, "I hope you didn't stop on the way to do a bit of 'fishing'!"
Donald John laughed, "Och, away with you woman, I wouldn't do such a thing with the Meenister on board! It was the two lovebirds canoodling that held us back!"

Rhona blushed at the thought of a Meenister *canoodling*, and Mhàiri and Kirsty looked at each other and giggled.
"Stop that you two!" Rhona admonished her daughters. "Help the Meenister out of the boat. Kirsty, take the Meenisters case!"

"Ochón, Meenister, the young generation!" Rhona said to Colin, shaking her head.
"It's no wonder the grey hairs are beginning to come through, and me a young woman in my prime too!"

Donald John coughed rather too loudly and Rhona gave him a 'look' which said, *'be careful now!'*

He looked at Colin and gave a smile and a wink.

Once Colin was safely onshore, Rhona said "Come away up to the croft Meenister, the kettle is on and I've made a fresh batch of treacle scones, I know they're your favourite."

"That sounds great Rhona, that will settle my stomach, just what I need.".

As they walked up to the croft, he looked around at the spectacular scenery.

Donald John and Rhona were chatting away in their native tongue, the two girls were chasing each other and laughing, and he felt the warmth of the sun on his face – and he knew that this was God's special place.

As they entered the croft, Colin's senses were arrested by the pungent, sweet aroma of a peat fire burning in the hearth.

"Sit yourself down Meenister," Rhona said, waving towards the big comfy chair beside the fire. "You've had quite a time of it, these past few days. Here's a wee dram and a scone, just put your feet up relax for a wee while."

Had it only been a few days since all this began? It seemed so much longer.
He remembered the day that the letter from the Oban solicitor had arrived, which led him to think of his wee pal Moses – and then his mind wandered on to his pride and joy – his motorbike, his 1938, 500 cc BSA Goldstar.

When his head was in a muddle, he would often take a run out on his motorbike, across Glasgow and up through Alexandria and away up Loch Lomond side to his favourite place, the beautiful wee village of Luss, where he would sit and look out over the Loch and ponder the various issues which bothered him. Once his mind was clearer, he would ride home to his flat in Kelvinside for a nice cup of tea and a custard cream biscuit.
But all that seemed so far away in both time and distance.

As he thought on all these things, the sea air, the large glass of Jura Malt whisky and the warmth from the peat fire lulled him into closing his eyes and before he knew it, he was fast asleep.

But after a time, his sleep was visited by a dream which saw Colin at sea in a small boat. He had lost both oars and was drifting helplessly. The waves were getting higher and the sea seemed as if it was becoming more angry with each wave.

He was feeling anxious, helpless and out of control, tossing this way and that as if two pairs of unseen hands were pulling him in opposite directions.

After what seemed like an age of struggling and tussling, Colin heard a distant voice saying, "Meenister, Meenister, it is myself." Was it a dream or was it real? Colin couldn't be sure, but then he felt a hand on his shoulder, was it the saving hand of God, or a more sinister grasp intent on dragging him down to the unseen depths below?

His mind was racing and as he sat bolt upright,

his hands gripped the arms of the chair and beads of sweat were on his brow.

His eyes opened to see Donald John standing beside him saying, "Meenister, Meenister, it is only myself, Rhona says that dinner is ready, and you are to come through to the kitchen before it gets cold."

Colin was still shaking from his unsettling dream but managed to say, "Oh...yes, of course." But it took a few moments before he could compose himself enough to stand and walk through to the kitchen.

His heart was warmed at the sight of Rhona at the cooker and Kirsty and Mhàiri sitting at the table with a space between them, both saying, "Here Meenister, come and sit here."

"Now, girls, don't be harassing the Meenister!" to which they replied in unison, "Yes mother."

"Never mind them, Meenister, sit yourself down."

"Over here!" the girls said excitedly as they patted the chair between them, and to their joy Colin obliged and joined them at the table, sitting in between them.

A large pot of Lamb stew was laid in the centre of the table and two large bowls of steaming boiled potatoes, with their skins still on, were placed beside it. The sight and the smells were enough to make Colin's mouth water, quite literally.

The girls lifted up their forks ready to strike out at the potatoes, but their father stopped them in their tracks. "Girls!" Donald John said firmly. "You know better than that!"

"Yes father," the girls replied and put down their forks.

"Meenister, would you put up a Grace for us?" Donald John asked.

"Yes of course. Such a magnificent display of God's good provision for his people," Colin remarked as he surveyed the table of food laid before them.

He asked them to hold hands around the table, forming a 'family circle'.

As Colin took a hand of both of the girls, one on either side, they looked over at each other, and went bright red.

Colin said Grace and they all said, 'Amen.'

# Chapter 25

*"Now don't you be quizzing the Meenister,"*
*said Uisdean to his wife with a wink,*
*"He has his 'Clerical discrechency' to think of!"*

◆

"I love tatties with their jackets still on," Donald
John said as he served Colin a generous portion
from a bowl of steaming potatoes.

"Me too," agreed Colin and he smiled at Donald
John's remarks.

He would never hear such comments in the
upmarket area of Kelvinside in Glasgow where he
lived, indeed there were many other things that
he had seen, heard and experienced over the past
few days or so which would have been
completely alien in Glasgow, but of course, he
was in the Inner Hebrides now – it was like a
different world - and how grateful he was for that.

*'The Lord is good indeed,'* he thought to himself and
tucked into the most tasty, mouth watering meal
he could ever remember eating. Good company
and good food, who could ask for more?

After dinner, Rhona and the girls cleared up while Colin and Donald John sat with a dram, putting the world to rights.

Their conversation ranged from, 'The Roman Empire,' to Donald John's declaration that 'a good pair of boots is a great thing.'

At some point in the evening the neighbours, Uisdean (*oost-yan*) and his wife Donalda, came in and brought more food and an extra bottle of Whisky, just incase.

After a dram or two, Rhona sang a beautiful Gaelic song which brought a tear to Colin's eyes as it reminded him of how much he was missing Lorna.

The girls, Mhàiri and Kirsty, sang Gaelic songs and showed their prowess at the Highland dancing as Uisdean played his Melodeon and Donalda accompanied him on the 'Jews harp,' or 'Trump' as it is often called in those parts.

Donald John recited an old Gaelic poem that he had learned at school, believed to be written by the early Bard, Ossian, steeped in mythological imagery.

Uisdean and Donalda seemed to know all about Colin and Lorna's romance and when Colin asked how they knew, Donalda simply said, "The jungle drums have been beating!" and gave Colin a wink.

Then she asked Colin if it was true that he had drunk the Free Kirk Minister under the table at the Wake. Colin was quite taken aback. *He was still embarrassed by the whole business - which, by the way, was to be told and retold so many times over the years that it raised Colin's status to that of 'local hero' in certain circles.*

"Now don't you be quizzing the Meenister," said Uisdean to his wife with a wink, "he has his 'Clerical discrechency to think of!"

"Aye," said Donald John, "Do Meenisters not have to keep everything secret?"

"That's Priests at confessionals, ya daft old bodach!" said Rhona.

"Aye, well..." Colin blustered, and remembered

that there was something in his room that he had to go and check.

However, all in all, it was a great night, or at least as far as Colin could remember.

He woke the next morning, Saturday, with a bit of a headache. As he walked through to the kitchen, he found Rhona busy making scones on the girdle.

"Good morning Meenister, how's the head this morning?" she asked.

"It's a bit groggy Rhona, it must have been something I ate last night," he replied.

"Aye, that would be it," Rhona smiled.

"And please, Rhona, call me Colin."

"Calling the Meenister by his first name, I could never do that, it's disrespectful!"

"But I like to think that I am more than just 'the Minister' to you and your lovely family. Am I not a friend too?"

"Yes, of course you are."

"And don't friends call each other by their first names?"

"Yes, you are right, of course – Colin," and she emphasized his name as she spoke.

"There, that wasn't so hard, was it?" A warm glow came over him, making him feel very much a part of this lovely family.

Donald John came in rubbing his head and looking very off colour. "Have you any ENO's Liver salts, mo ghràdh *(mo grai - my love)*?" he asked Rhona.

"Aye, the tin is in the press, there should be some left after Hogmanay, and would you make up a glass for Colin too?"

"Who in Jehovah's name is Colin?" Donald John asked.

"It's Colin, the Meenister, ya daft lump!"

"Aye, but.. but.. is it not disrespectful to call the Meenister by his first name?"

"Och, Donald John, it's old fashioned that you are!"

"Oh yes, Donald John, it's okay." Colin felt he should come to Rhona's aid. "I asked Rhona to call me Colin, after all, am I not a friend of the family?"

"You are indeed... but..." Donald John stuttered.

"Well, there you are then," Rhona said with a grin and a wink to Colin.

Donald John could see he was outnumbered and so he put two spoonful's of the Liver Salts into each of the two glasses, added water and a dash of whisky in to each of them, stirred them and said, "Here, Meenister, sorry… Colin, that will put hairs on your chest!" as he handed Colin one glass and drunk the other down in one go.

"Mercy! You can't be saying things like that to a Meenister!" Rhona said sharply.

"Och, it's okay my sweet, it's only our good friend Colin." Donald John smiled sweetly at Rhona and walked out of the room.

The rest of the day was a lazy day, the girls took Colin for a walk around the village and introduced him to all the local characters they met.

There was Duncan the Post, Murdo the fish man, Mary Beth the Postmistress and Robert MacIlvaney the road sweep, affectionally known as Bob the Brush.

They met the Head Teacher of the local school, Mr. Cunningham, and one of the teachers, Mr MacDonald, who was out getting his messages (*shopping*) who was otherwise known as, 'the Haddie.'

It was a lovely morning and Colin enjoyed just ambling around the village, chatting to the locals and admiring the beautiful scenery.
The girls were a delight, full of fun and mischief, giggling and nudging each other over some secret joke that only they shared.

Colin spotted Donald John and Uisdean carrying what looked like petrol cans down to the boat, and wondered, *'what are those two rascals up to?'*
Whatever it was, he was sure they were up to no good.

The evening was a quiet but pleasant affair, and a dram or two was taken, just to be sociable.
Uisdean's wife, Donalda, sang a number of beautiful Gaelic songs and Donald John regaled them with stories and jokes which caused much hilarity.
Uisdean showed himself to be quite the story teller. He spoke in a low, sombre voice as he told the, 'Tale of the headless horseman of Tiree' - and

the fascinating story of a seal who changed into a beautiful girl and married a local lad.

They had a child they called "Lilly' and then she changed back into a seal and returned to the sea, taking the child with her, neither of whom were ever seen again.

Colin smiled as he looked over and saw Mhairi and Kirsty holding on to each other, wide eyed and taking in every word.

The drams were flowing and the craic was good, Colin had loved every minute of it.

It hadn't been a late night but it was a good old fashioned, Island 'Ceilidh'.

# Chapter 26

*"Aye, God is good indeed," said Murdo the Postie,*
*a sentiment which was shared by all."*

◆

It was Sunday morning, the Sabbath day.
Over breakfast, Rhona asked Donald John what his plans were for the day.

"Well, um… Uisdean and I were thinking of maybe, perhaps, er…taking the Meenister, sorry, Colin, over to the mainland. The Oban ferry doesn't come until Tuesday, it'll get him home all the sooner, did I not say?"
This was news to Colin.

"No, you did not!" Rhona's suspicions were aroused. "What are you two rascals up to!?"
"Och, nothing at all sweetheart," said Donald John in his most angelic voice.

"But it's the Sabbath," Rhona was surprised as Donald John would never take the boat out on a Sunday. He would wait until one minute after midnight on the Monday morning before going out to sea but never during the 24 hours of the Sabbath.

"Well, as you know, we wouldn't usually go out on the Sabbath day but as it's for a 'man of the cloth' that's needing to get home - it would be a kind of 'mission of mercy,' would it not?"

"Rhona shook her head and was about to speak when their neighbour Uisdean knocked, walked in and said, 'What time are we leaving Donald John? I've got the last of the fish boxed up and on the boat."
Rhona gave Donald John one of her 'looks' which said, *'What in mercy's name is going on!?'*

Uisdean spoke up in Donald John's defence, "We went out for an hour or so last night to do a bit of 'night fishing,' it was before 12 o'clock," he emphasised, "and we had a bumper catch.
Donald John had the great idea to take the Meenister over to Oban and while we were there we could sell our catch too. The hotels are paying good money for the fish just now, the towerists

can't get enough of them! They're eating them for breakfast, dinner and tea!"

"Are they now?" Rhona was not best pleased with the idea.

Uisdean said, "Wait you..." and went out to the boat and returned carrying a fine sized fish.

"I almost forgot, here's a bonnie Sea Trout for you Rhona. I know you are partial to a nice piece of Sea Trout, tastier than Salmon I always say."

Colin sat watching and listening to this almost surreal conversation, not least because after everyone had gone off to bed last night, Donald John and Uisdean had gone out fishing!

"What a pair of rogues you are!" Rhona said, "But the sea trout will make a lovely fish pie for myself and the girls while you are away galavanting over to Oban. What am I to do with you two?" Rhona was used to the escapades of her husband and his good friend Uisdean. This latest ploy was by no means the worst of it.

"What time are you leaving?"

"With the tide at 10 o'clock," Donald John replied.

"Well, you better get a move on, it's after 9 now!" Rhona said.

Donald John looked over at Uisdean and gave him a furtive smile.

"And don't you be smiling, Donald John! You'll pay for this, I haven't worked out how just yet, but be sure I *will* find a way!" Rhona turned and gave Colin a smile and a wink as she took the sea trout through to the scullery.

\*

Meanwhile, back on Rhua, the island's GP and Session Clerk, Doctor Eustace Killmennie, had been approached by a good number of people, all asking the same question – "Could we ask the Reverend Colin Campbell if he would come and be the Minister of the Church on Rhua?" He was in total agreement and determined to take it further.

So, before the Sunday Service began, he had asked the Rev McCrimmond if he could have a few words with the congregation at the end of the service.

The service was an hour and a half of McCrimmond reminding the congregation that they were all sinners and destined for a fiery eternity if they did not give their lives over to Jesus.

It was a strong, well intended message, however, many had already accepted that Divine invitation and had spent the service counting the number of panes of glass in the church windows.

There were four windows, two on each side of the church, each with eight rows of six small panes, giving forty-eight small panes per window. Four times forty-eight equals one hundred and ninety-two panes.

It had been counted by many people over many years and the answer was always the same, one hundred and ninety-two, yet congregations continue to count them, especially through the Reverend McCrimmond's dry, lengthy sermons.

At the end of the Service, Dr Killmennie rose to speak and there was an air of expectancy as the congregation wondered what it was all about.

"Reverend McCrimmond, brothers and sisters," he said in a serious and solemn voice. He was revelling in his 'moment' and was determined to impress the gravity of his words upon all who were listening (and were not busy counting the window panes).

It was, to be fair, a significant moment in the life of the church as they had not had the opportunity to discuss the possibility of a Minister for 10 years.

Dr Killmennie outlined the many positive comments he had received and closed his short speech to the congregation with a question, well, two questions. 1. "Are you in agreement that you would like the Reverend Colin Campbell to be our Minister? and 2. Do you instruct me to pursue the matter with the Reverend Campbell?"

The church erupted with shouts of, "Yes! Hurray!"

Reverend McCrimmond felt uneasy with so much joy and general happiness being expressed in the Lord's house on the Sabbath day – but the thought of having a colleague to share the Church Services and general Parish duties of the Island, appealed to him very much and before he knew it, he found himself clapping too!

Seeing Reverend McCrimmond clapping brought a great cheer from the congregation.

Once it had all calmed down, Dr Killmennie asked for the Elders to stay behind to arrange a meeting to get things moving.

Outside the Church there was a buzz as people chatted excitedly at the thought of having such a young (and good looking) Minister after all these years.

It was agreed that this was surely an answer to their prayers.

"Aye, God is good indeed," said Murdo the Post, a sentiment which was shared by all.

A small group of Elders met in the church hall after the service and Dr Killmennie opened the meeting with prayer. He then explained that it was an informal meeting to get the ball rolling.

He said that if everyone agreed, he would contact the Church of Scotland Head office and seek advice how to proceed.

The Elders were excited (*in as much as Church of Scotland Elders can get excited*) and it was unanimously agreed that Dr Killmennie should go ahead and get things moving.

After a general discussion, he said he would contact Head Office in Edinburgh in the morning and would call another Elders meeting once he knew more.

The Elders left in high spirits, all hoping and praying that Colin would soon be their Minister.

.

*

Over on Coll, Donald John and Uisdean went down to the shore prepare the 'Donalda Dream' for their trip over to Oban, while Colin followed Rhona into the scullery.

"Donald John certainly keeps you on your toes, Rhona!" said Colin.

"Aye, he does that," Rhona remarked, "but he's harmless really and he's a good father to the girls, even tho' he hasn't much of a clue. He was brought up on the croft by his father and with 3 brothers, so the ways of women are pretty much a mystery to him but I'm getting him trained up." Colin laughed and said, "Well, you're doing a good job."

"Aye, so far... it's a 'work in progress' as you might say."

The girls, Mhàiri and Kirsty, had been on a sleep-over at their friends along the road and Rhona had sent word that they were to come home straight away.

Before long, they were all back in the croft chatting over tea and home made scones. Colin looked around the room – it was a simple home yet so full of love and laughter.

Donald John and Rhona were the salt of the earth, Mhàiri and Kirsty were lovely girls who had not yet been changed by the ways of the outside world and Uisdean and Donalda were the kind of people that everyone would be pleased to have as neighbours.

He felt a pang of sorrow as he thought of leaving this idyllic place – which was soon followed by a warm glow and a feeling of 'belonging' in this wonderful part of God's creation.

Uisdean's wife Donalda, popped in with a bag of freshly baked cheese scones and a Thermos flask of tea for the boat journey, along with a note of some parcels which were waiting to be picked up at the Oban bus station before the 'boys' returned home.

# Chapter 27

*"A decent haul of fish, a good friend, a song and a dram, could it get any better?..."*

◆

The time had come, it was 10 am and the tide was beginning to turn. "Well, it's time to be setting off," Donald John said.

"Aye, Donald John," said Uisdean, "but it still doesn't feel right, going out on the Sabbath day."

"It's a mission of mercy that we are on, the good Lord will watch over us. And besides, we'll have the Meenister on board, what harm can come to us?"

Uisdean wasn't completely convinced.

One by one, the group took it in turns to give Colin a hug.

"Well, Meenister, sorry, Colin, you have fair made an impression on us all and we will surely miss you." Donald John felt the tears begin to well up in his eyes as he spoke.

"Be sure and come back and see us – and perhaps you would offer up a prayer before we leave?"

Colin was struggling to hold back the tears too.

"Yes, of course," Colin answered. Everyone bowed their head and he prayed for God's loving care to watch over each of them – and for a safe journey as Uisdean's boat carried them over the waters to Oban, and to return Donald John and Uisdean home safely to their families. He prayed that by God's grace, they would all meet again one day – and they all said, "Amen."

By the time he had finished the prayer they were all in tears and Donald John sniffed and made for the door, lifting Colin's case and coat on his way out.

"Be sure to come back and see us Colin," Rhona said tearfully.

"Yes, you *must* come back," said Mhàiri and Kirsty in unison and ran into their bedroom in tears.

"I'm going to miss you all too, and I promise that I *will* be back."  Colin then gave Rhona another hug. "Thank you Rhona, you are a very special lady with a very special family, may God bless you all."

Colin felt that if he didn't leave now, he might never leave, so he turned, left the cottage, crossed the road and walked along the path to the Pier, where the Donalda Dream was tied up - taking in the salty scent of the sea as he went.

As he looked back he saw the family group following him. Mhàiri and Kirsty ran down and took an arm each and walked beside him for the last few yards to Uisdean's boat.

The 'Donalda Dream' was 21 feet long, painted pale blue and white with a small cab up front, whereas Donald John's small boat was basically a rowing boat with an outdated outboard engine.

"Now be sure and get on the boat with the right foot first," Kirsty said to Colin.
"But which one is the 'right' foot, the left or the right?" Colin said with a grin.
"The RIGHT foot silly!" said Mhàiri patting her right leg. "It's for a safe crossing."
Colin remembered what the Porter on Oban Pier had said, *"Be sure to get on with the right foot."* Now it made sense. Far from being a dark foreboding warning, the old salt was, in fact, wishing Colin a safe journey.

The girls untied the ropes and it didn't take long before the tearful little group waving from the shore, were just specks on the coastline.

There was a mild breeze and as always, for this part of the world, the possibility of a shower or two was never far away.

Colin was spellbound by the beauty which was all around him. He knew the dramatic scenery around Rannoch Moor and Glencoe from his climbing trips with his pal Iain McDougall – but this was a different kind of beauty. It was open, serene and yet wild and untamed at the same time. Colin thought, *'It is just so beautiful, how can anyone deny the Creator's hand at work here?'*

Donald John and Uisdean were at the wheel, chatting, laughing and singing in their native tongue. They were in their element, at sea with a decent haul of fish, a good friend, a song and a dram, could it get any better?

Colin couldn't remember ever seeing two such happy and contented friends.

They had been at sea for about half an hour when Uisdean shouted, "Look Meenister – basking sharks, do you see them?" as he pointed out to sea.

Colin struggled to see anything except water and more water, but as he narrowed his eyes and focused, he spotted a number of sharks, relaxing in the sunshine just a few hundred yards away.

"I see them! I see them!" Colin shouted excitedly. Donald John handed him an old leather bound telescope. "You'll see them better with this. Look along the top of it and point it towards the sharks and then look through the lense." Colin scanned the waves for a few minutes and then he saw them in close up. "Goodness me!" Colin shouted, "they're just so...." He was lost for words at the splendour of it all.

"And don't be surprised if we're joined by a school of dolphins," Donald John said to Colin. "They like to swim alongside us, but they're friendly enough."

"Will… will they not overturn us!?" Colin was alarmed at the thought of being capsized so far from land.

"Och not at all," said Uisdean. "They'll not do us any harm, they enjoy the company," and he smiled at Donald John.

Before long, land could be seen off their starboard side. "That's Mull you can see over there," Uisdean said. "And if you look over to your left, on the Port side, you'll see the Treshnish Islands – can you see the one that looks a hat? It's known as the Dutchman's cap, can you see it?"

Colin struggled to make out an island that resembled a hat, but then he saw it, it seemed to jump out at him. It was a long flat landscape with a rounded hump in the centre. "Yes, yes, I see it now, it's amazing, just like a large Panama hat from the side!"

Colin's eyes weren't attuned to recognizing such things, not like Donald John and Uisdean, they were men of the land and sea, being brought up to see and appreciate the wonders of nature in all its raw, natural beauty.

However, one sense that still served Colin well was his sense of smell.

The boxes of fish and lobsters, as well as the nets and the creels which covered the deck, all gave off a pungent aroma which would turn the stomach of the strongest landlubber. Lobsters were crawling out of their boxes in a bid to escape captivity and the salt water swirled around the bottom of the boat.

Colin was kept busy putting them back in their open top boxes, only for them to attempt another breakout.

Soon the 'Donalda Dream' was turning into the Sound of Mull, down past Ardmore Point, and by Tobermory.

They saw a number of grey seals lounging on the rocks as they went on past the old wooden Pier at Craignure, then on by Duart Castle, the 13th century seat of Clan MacLean, and then across the Firth of Lorne and into the safe haven of Oban Bay.

# Chapter 28

*"You'll know if the Po-lis is coming, you'll hear his bi-cycle squeaking, that's why they call him 'Squeaker'..."*

◆

Meanwhile, back in Rhua, Dr Killmennie had sent a Telegram to the Church of Scotland Offices in Edinburgh first thing on Monday morning and to his great surprise, had received a reply later the same day.

He managed to contact the Elders and arranged a meeting that very evening to tell them the news. Things were moving a pace!

it was a cold, dreich evening as the Elders made their way to the Kirk Session meeting in the church hall, but their spirits were high.

The Elders were excited to hear the positive response from Head Office.

A letter would follow with further information, but meantime they were given permission to contact Reverend Colin Campbell to invite him up for interview.

They talked it through and after much discussion, they drafted out a letter to Colin which Dr Killmennie asked his good lady, who was acting 'ex officio', to read out.

"Of course, Mr Chairman," she said to her husband. "I'll have to tidy it up a bit here is the gist of it."

She cleared her throat as if to read some weighty passage of Scripture on a Sunday morning and began.

*"Dear Reverend Campbell, at a recent meeting of the Kirk Session of Rhua Parish Church, as dated above, it was unanimously agreed that you be invited to come for an interview regarding the Post of Parish Minister of Rhua Parish Church of Scotland.*

*In order to expedite this matter, you are invited to telephone the Session Clerk, Dr. Eustace Killmennie on telephone number Rhua 24 to arrange further proceedings, at your earliest convenience.'*

*Yours in anticipation etc."*

*P.S. If the phone line does not connect, please try later as the mast is often blown over by the wind and the sheep chew the connections.*

Dr Killmennie asked the group, "Do we all agree that this letter be sent to the Reverend Campbell?" He looked around the table to see each head nod in agreement - even Murdo the Postie who usually disagreed on some minor point as a matter of principle, nodded his head.

"Okay then, as per your instruction, I will communicate this to the Rev Campbell and call a further meeting when I receive his reply, to make any further arrangements as necessary."
Dr. Killmennie thanked all for their attendance and closed the meeting with prayer.

The Elders stood around outside talking excitedly about how much they wanted Colin to be their Minister.
One Elder said, "Oh I do hope he accepts, what a tonic he will be for our congregation."
"Yes" said another, looking around, "He'll be a breath of fresh air for the Island – a fair change from the doom and gloom of Mr McCrimmond!"

*

In Oban, the 'Donalda Dream' was safely tied up at the North Pier and Donald John and Uisdean set-to and off-loaded the boxes of fish onto a trolley that was lying on the Pier.

"My cousin's man from Barra, Donnie, is a chef at the 'Highland Tartan Hotel' he's always looking for fresh fish, he'll give us a good price," said Uisdean.

So, the two of them wheeled the haul of fish around to the back door of the Hotel while Colin was delegated to watch out for the local constabulary.

"You'll know if the Po-lis is coming, you'll hear his bi-cycle squeaking, that's why they call him 'Squeaker' – you can hear him before you see him!" Donald John explained.

Uisdean stuck his head into the kitchen door of the hotel and shouted in Gaelic, "Is that rogue Donnie McAskill still masquerading as a cook in these parts!?"

"Oh, it's yourself!" a voice replied, "What brings you over to civilization you rascal?" It was

Donnie, a short, heavy set, dark haired man with a smile that would light up any room.

"How is Margaret?" Uisdean asked.

"Still complaining," replied Donnie.

"Just the usual then," said Uisdean with a smile.

After exchanging pleasantries, Donnie asked, "What brings you here? As if I need to ask."

"We have a bumper haul for you. We saved the best quality fish for yourself, seeing as you are the finest chef in all of Oban and have your reputation to think of."

"Well, I'll not contradict you there," Donnie replied, "but don't think that your flattery will get you a better price!"

"Oh, mercy no, nothing was further from my mind!" Uisdean pretended to be hurt by Donnie's remarks.

"Ok, what have you got for us?"

Uisdean and Donald John carried in the boxes of fish along with two large boxes of Lobsters.

"Oh, hello Donald John," Donnie was pleased to see his old friend. "You're in bad company today with this scoundrel!" he said and nodded towards

Uisdean. They all smiled and Donnie went through the haul.

"Aye, you have a fair catch I'll give you that. The towerists will make short work of them."

"Oh, is that so?" Uisdean pretended to be surprised.

"Well, I never, isn't it just the good fortune that we kept the best quality for yourself. You'll be run-over with the holiday makers once the word gets out!"

"Did the Squeaker see you? The boys were saying that he is out on the prowl today," Donnie asked. He liked to keep himself above suspicion but little did he know that he was well known to the local Police.

"No Donnie, we kept to the back streets for safety."

"Ok Uisdean, so how much are you wanting for the lot?"

"Oh, just a fair price, that's all we ask for. Aye, a fair price."

After some haggling a 'fair' price was agreed and Donald John and Uisdean left the hotel with a wad of cash in hand, quite forgetting that Colin was waiting outside.

"Oh Meenister! Sorry to have left you outside, but my cousin's man is funny about Meenisters. Fair knocks him for six when he sees them.
His dear mother, God rest her soul, used to cross the road when a Meenister was coming - and if he spoke to her, she would turn around three times and spit."
"Oh dear," said Colin in his best highland accent. "We wouldn't want that would we? Especially with all that spitting."
Uisdean and Donald John fell silent, not sure if Colin was being serious or pulling their legs with his, 'Highland Meenisterial impreshination,' as Uisdean called it.
"Aye, just that," Donald John and Uisdean said in unison.
"Well, I'll have to make my way down to Glasgow but I'm not sure if the buses run on Sunday," said Colin.
"I'll go into the Bar and ask about the buses." Uisdean said, "I'd better come with you," said

Donald John, "Just incase."

'Incase of what?' Colin wondered.

Ten minutes later and with a strong smell of whisky on their breath, they returned with both bad and good news.

"It looks like you are out of luck Meenister, there is not another bus going down to Glasgow today, but there is good news too!

There's a lorry driver in the Bar just now, a good Tiree man, and he's taking a wee refreshment before heading down to Glasgow to pick up a load at the market in the morning, and he is willing to give you a lift."

Alarm bells rang in Colin's mind. Thoughts of a lorry driver drinking in a Bar and then driving down to Glasgow didn't appeal to him.

Did he really want to chance it? But what else was he to do?

"Or you could spend the night in the Deep Sea

Fisherman's Mission over by the Pier," Uisdean suggested, failing to mention that they weren't too keen on Minister's there either.

# Chapter 29

*"His own mother was as good a Christian woman as
ever there was, as humble as the good Lord himself..."*

◆

Colin decided to take the lorry driver up on his
kind offer. After all, would the good Lord not be
with him? At least he would be home and in his
own bed tonight – and his wee pal Moses would
curl up on the covers beside him. The thought of
it made him keen to get home.

Out of courtesy and perhaps the thought of a wee
dram to be sociable, Uisdean and Donald John
went round to the bar with Colin, just to keep him
company.
"Don't be worrying Colin, we'll just be having the
one drink and we will be on our way too," said
Donald John as he led the way round to the Public
Bar.

"But I thought that the pubs were all closed on a
Sunday?" Colin said.
"Some of them are – but if you are a 'bona fide'
traveller you can get a drink. And as we have

travelled over from Rhua we wouldn't want to cause any offence by not taking a dram!"

They say that 'the world is a small place' and nowhere is that more true than in the Western Highlands and Islands of Scotland.

On entering the 'Bothy' Public Bar Donald John and Uisdean knew at least 6 people.

"Oh, look out boys!" one customer said loudly, "It's the Coll Mafia - and a Priest in tow to take their confessionals," much to the amusement of the 'boys' in the Bar.

Colin took umbrage at being mistaken for a Priest and said in a mock serious tone "Actually, I am a Church of Scotland Minister – and it's *them* that's keeping ME out of mischief!"

After a short pause, everyone laughed and someone said, "Aye, you'll do Meenister, you'll do."

Colin had instantly made a room full of friends.

A short, dark haired man in a greasy boiler suit

who was standing at the bar, smoking a roll-up cigarette, spoke to Colin. "Hello, you'll be the Meenister that's wanting a run down to Glasgow." It was more of a statement of fact than a question.

"Yes, that would be very kind of you, I seem to have missed the last bus."

"It's no problem, I'm going that way myself just shortly, ready for the market first thing tomorrow morning. Oh, where are my manners? My name is Harrold, Harrold with two RR's."

The name struck a chord with Colin but surely there can't be two Harrold's, could there?

"I believe you know my cousin who has the shop in Kinlochmhor on Rhua." Harrold said.

"Oh yes, he's quite a character isn't he? He loves his wee shop," said Colin.

"Don't be letting him hear you calling it a 'wee shop'!"

"Oh no, of course it's a - 'Grand Emporium'!" Colin said with a smile.

Harrold laughed. "Oh aye, he has always had the airs and graces, no-one knows where he gets them from. Not from his own mother anyway – as good a Christian woman as ever there was, as humble as the good Lord himself.

And I've heard through the grapevine that his daughter Lorna is winching a Meenister, would that be your good self?" Harrold asked with a mischievous smile.

Colin was quite taken aback – how on earth did word get over here so fast?

"She's a lovely lass, takes after her mother, salt of the earth," Harrold said.

"Oh yes, she is a lovely girl, indeed yes... er.. what time are we leaving for Glasgow, Harrold?" Colin asked, in the hope of changing the subject, but this was too good to let go, so Harrold continued, "Aye, her mother was always the belle of the ball, all the lads chased her but she was fly and kept them on a string, until she met my cousin Harrold at the dancing in Arinagour. Although I don't know what she saw in him, when there were plenty more young stags who would gladly have kept her company."

Harrold seemed to be up for a good blether but

Colin was keen on getting down the road but even more keen to change the topic of Harrold's conversation, so he interrupted by looking at his pocket watch and saying, "Oh goodness, look at the time, should we not be getting down the road?"

"Aye, maybe that," Harrold had to admit, and he finished his dram, stubbed out his cigarette in the ashtray on the bar and handed a 10 shilling note to the barman.

"Will I just keep the change Harrold?" the barman said, knowing well what the answer would be.

"Don't even think about it! You know fine well that I have 10 children to support – but don't let on to the wife!" The boys in the bar laughed as the barman handed over the loose change.

"Well, Meenister, we can't stay here blethering all day, we'll have to make our way down to the great metro-polis or the markets will be open by the time we get there."

Donald John and Uisdean, who were sitting at a table with some old friends, stood up and shook Colin's hand and wished him well.

All three agreed that they would meet again before too long.

The 100 mile or so journey down to Glasgow was a long and tedious one. Harrold's lorry was slow, noisy and rattled along the twisty roads – and to make matters worse, Harrold insisted on singing Gaelic songs which, to Colin's untrained ear, sounded like he was singing them all to the same soulful tune.

The last week had taken its toll on Colin and a wave of tiredness come over him.

Not only that, but he was also missing Lorna. It had all been a whirlwind and not in the least expected.

*'The Lord works in mysterious ways his wonders to perform,'* Colin said to himself, feeling quite sure that it was all part of a greater plan.

If that were so, then there was no point in fighting it, *'What will be will be,'* and he looked up, smiled and said quietly *'Thank you Lord,'* and drifted off to sleep.

Colin dozed on and off for most of the way, being woken only by the twists and turns of the road, more so after they had passed Tyndrum,

Crianlarich and travelled down Loch Lomond side.

Sudden jolts and abrupt braking meant Colin was tossed from side to side and back and forth, much to the amusement of Harrold.

"Aye, Meenister, you'll need to hold on tight, But it'll not be long before we'll be going by Tarbet and the road straightens out a bit from there on." He felt a sense of relief that he would soon be on familiar ground and in his own bed before too long.

As they came into the outskirts of Glasgow Harrold asked, "Where is it that you want dropping off Meenister? I can't be leaving you to walk the streets of Glasgow at night, you being a Meenister and all."

"That's very kind of you Harrold, I live in Kelvinside, so wherever is handy for you."
"That's no bother, I'll cut through Byers Road on to Dumbarton Road and I'll drop you off at the Kelvin Bridge, how would that suit you?"
"Yes, that would be great, I've only a five minute walk from there."

Soon they arrived at the magnificent Kelvin Bridge with its beautiful ironwork and ornate lamps.

As Colin climbed down from the cab, Harrold shouted, "Fare well Meenister – and when I'm home next I'll tell Lorna that you were asking kindly for her."

"Yes, please do, and thank you Harrold, it's been quite a.. um.. quite a journey,  and very much appreciated."

He stood on the roadside for a few minutes wondering if the whole population of the Highlands and Islands were related to each other.

What were the chances of a lorry driver he had met in a bar in Oban being related to Lorna MacDonald on the remote Island of Rhua?

Yes, the Islanders were a different breed from any other he had come across before, but for all that, they now had a very special place in his heart.

Within a few minutes Colin was standing at his

front door, it was good be home. His cat, Moses,

had appeared from out of somewhere and wrapped his tail around Colin's leg, purring loudly. He picked his wee pal up and carried him inside.

"It's good to be home," he said out loud, not knowing that Moses was thinking the very same thing.

# Chapter 30

*"I hope they're not too racy,"*
*said one of the ladies."*
*"I hope they are!" said another…"*

❖

The next morning, Colin was making a cup of tea when he heard the front door open, it was his housekeeper Mrs McRae.

"Oh, good Lord, what a fright you gave me Minister! It's usually Moses that greets me, but it's good to see you home safe and sound.

How was it up in the Hee-lands? You hear so many stories, don't you?"

Colin wasn't sure just what stories Mrs McRae was referring to. "Oh no Mrs McRae, it's just beautiful up there, so peaceful and the people are lovely too."

"Oh, well, you're home safe and sound and that's the main thing," Mrs McRae replied.

Suddenly realising that Colin was still in his pyjamas, she said, "I'll… em, go and set the fire," and she hurried through to the sitting room and began rolling up newspapers for fire-lighters.

Seeing the Minister in his pyjamas made her feel uncomfortable somehow, him being a man of the cloth.

Colin washed and dressed before going through to his study to sort out the letters which had arrived in his absence.

He smiled as he sat at his desk. Mrs McRae had laid out the post into two piles, white envelopes and brown envelopes, knowing that Colin always chose to open them in that order. *'Nothing gets past dear Mrs McRae,'* he thought.

He looked around at the familiar family photos, his many books and the pictures of Glencoe which hung on his study wall, all recalling happy memories.

Just then, Moses jumped up onto his lap, cooried in and purred loudly.

It was good to be back home with all his own familiar things around him.

\*

It was nine o'clock on Monday morning as Mr MacDonald opened up his Emporium.

He was his usual cheerful self, looking forward to a good day of serving the good people of Rhua.

Lorna, however, sat in the office, feeling sad. It had only been a few days since Colin had left Rhua but it seemed so much longer.
Would she ever see him again? Would he keep in touch as he said he would?

These and many other fears and concerns ran through her head.
"Come on now Lorna, don't be moping about, there's work to be done," her father said, trying to cheer his daughter up.

"There is that bundle of new flannelette nightgowns to be sorted out and put on display. The nights will be getting chillier soon and we might have a big rush on them!"
"Yes father," replied Lorna.
"We don't want the ladies of Rhua to be catching their death of cold now do we?"
"No father."

Lorna stirred herself and went through to the shop. There were already a few ladies in the shop browsing in the 'latest thing from Oban' section.

"Morning Lorna," one of the ladies said.

"Good morning, Mrs Ireland," Lorna answered. "Would you like to see the latest nightgowns, just in from Oban? They're so new that I haven't even had time to put them out on display."

"Oh, that would be great Lorna. I was just saying to Mrs Chisholm that the nights are fair drawing in."

"They certainly are," Lorna agreed as she brought the bundle of nightgowns through from the back of the shop. The ladies gathered round, excited to see what 'the latest thing from Oban' had to offer.

"I hope they're not too racy," said one of the ladies.

"I hope they are!" said another which caused great hilarity among the small group of ladies, including Lorna.

Her father looked proudly at his daughter. *'That's my girl,'* he thought. *"It's good to see her smile again, she's just as beautiful as her mother."*

*

It was Colin's first full day home. He started off by getting in touch with aunty Bunty and a few friends to let them know that he was home.

Mrs McRae was pleased with her gift of the tea cosy in the shape of a West Highland Terrier and couldn't wait to get home to try it out.

He opened a new packet of custard creams, made himself a cup of tea and went through to this study. His thoughts turned to Lorna and the future. As glad as he was to be home, he missed dear Lorna so very much.

Colin was happy they had agreed to keep in touch, but on returning from his Island trip he wondered just how practical that would be, long term. What to do?

Popping up to Rhua a couple of times a year wasn't really an option, he would miss Lorna too much in between visits.

Would he move up there permanently, after all they *were* looking for a Minister, would he apply for the job? But what if they said 'no'?

What if he moved up to Rhua and things didn't work out with Lorna?

Would he be better staying in Glasgow? If he did, would Lorna come down and live here? But how could he ask her to give up her family and move down to the big city? What if it didn't work out between them? How would he feel then? Lorna would have to move back to Rhua and that would be awful for her.

And there was the matter of his grandparent's Croft on Rhua. It was certainly a lovely place to live, but if he *were* to stay in the Central belt would it not be better to sell it?
And how would he do that? Who would handle the sale in such a remote location? How much should he ask for it?

So many questions were spinning around in his head, and he felt his stress levels rise. It wasn't like him as he was normally calm and collect in the face of difficult decisions, but all this seemed to be affecting him more than he had expected.

Extreme circumstances call for extreme measures, another cup of tea and two custard creams were required!

As he sat enjoying his tea and biscuits, his mind drifted back to thoughts of dear Lorna.

She was everything he imagined a girlfriend (or was it, 'wife'?) should be. Kind, caring, intelligent, funny, attractive as well as being supportive of his faith and calling to the Ministry. But sadly, she was a couple of hundred miles and a large expanse of water away.

All this was running through his mind when the communal phone rang in the hallway.

Another tenant answered and shouted – "Colin, it's for you. It's a young lady, so don't keep her waiting, Romeo!"

He wondered if it might be Lorna, she wasn't due to call until 7pm but if it *was* her, and he had a feeling that it was, what would he say? Should he tell her that he was thinking of applying for the post of Minister in Rhua? What would she think about that? Was it too forward, too soon? After all they had only met for the first time a few days ago.

Had he really thought it all through? Just a week or so ago he was sure that Glasgow was where God wanted him to be.

Oh dear – panic was setting in again.

He went out into the hallway and picked up the receiver. "Hello, Colin Campbell speaking, it is yourself Lorna?" he asked in as light hearted a voice as he could summon up.

"Yes, it's me." Lorna was tearful.

"I hope I'm not being a nuisance, but I just *had* to call, I couldn't wait until tonight. I'm missing you _so_ much! Did you get home alright? I was so worried!" Lorna chattered at double speed.

"Slow down sweetheart," Colin said. "Everything is alright – and I'm missing you too."

They spent the next few minutes talking about their feelings for each other and agreed that they both envisaged a future together, which was good news for Colin as it would help in his decision making process. Lorna was beyond happy as she now knew that Colin felt the same as her and a future with this lovely man was not just a dream. Time to make plans!

She was stirred from her daydream by hearing the pips going, reminding her that more money was needed or they would shortly be cut off.
Colin heard them too. "Where are you calling from, is it the hotel phone?"
"Yes, but I'm running out of coins."
"Don't worry darling, I'll speak to you tonight...."
They were just about to say their goodbyes when the line went dead.

Colin instinctively pressed button B in the hope that some loose change might drop down into the tray - but no luck, and he shrugged his shoulders and thought, *'Oh well, it's worth a try,'* and went back into his flat, to be greeted by Moses who wrapped himself around Colin's legs.

He was feeling emotional and couldn't hold back the tears. He lifted up Moses up and held him close to his chest.

Moses seemed to sense Colin's melancholy mood

and snuggled in and purred even louder.

*'Moses always knows when I'm sad,'* he thought to himself. *'He's a great wee pal.'*

# Chapter 31

*"In Safe Hands…"*

◆

As Colin sat with Moses on his knee, he couldn't stop thinking about his future with Lorna, but the same things kept going round and round in his mind and he felt he was getting nowhere, so he decided that he had to get up and go out to clear his head.

He thought he would go for a walk across to the Kelvingrove Art Gallery and Museum which was only a five minute walk from his flat.

It was a fascinating place where he had spent many hours studying and reflecting, during his student days.

He took a Thermos flask of tea, a small bottle of milk and a packet of custard creams and spent the rest of the afternoon walking around the museum and gallery.

He weighed up the options and what the best way to move forward in their relationship might be – and by the time he got back to his flat, he had formulated an outline of a rough plan.

It seemed no time before the clock struck 7pm. The butterflies began to take flight as he prepared to speak to Lorna.

As he was putting his plan into some kind of order in his mind, the phone rang. His heart started to race and he found himself shaking.

His nerves were getting the better of him.

"Hello sweetheart, how have you been today?" Colin asked.

"I've been busy in the shop with father, it makes the day go quicker."

"Oh right. That's good then…"

Lorna sensed that he wasn't his usual self.

"Are you alright Colin? Is everything okay?"

"Yes, everything is fine here – just missing you so much and I have such a lot going around in my head right now.

I love you, I really do and I want to spend the rest of my life with you, there, I said it! But there are so many things for us to think about."

Lorna was deliriously happy, as that was exactly what *she* wanted too, but she was concerned that Colin seemed to be stressed out about it all.

"And I want to spend the rest of my life with you too Colin, that's all that matters, please don't stress yourself about it – we *will* work it out. Love always finds a way, doesn't it?" Lorna said in a soothing voice.

Feeling calmer, Colin agreed, "You're quite right sweetheart. But how *can* we be together with me down here and you away up there?
I wouldn't ask you to move down here, you have your mother to think about and the shop and the way of life you are used to, it wouldn't be fair.

I've been thinking and have come up with a rough plan. Perhaps another option is…" he paused…
"If *I* were to move up to Rhua? How would you feel about that? I could apply for the post of Minister, but what if they didn't want me?"

Lorna had been in church when Dr Killmennie had asked the congregation if they wanted Colin to be their Minister. There had been cheering and clapping. They all agreed that he was the man for the job, and so did Lorna.
"Oh Colin, that would be wonderful! Of course

they would want you! You're the best Minister in the whole world, everyone says so!"

She was careful not to mention the business in the church, better to wait for the Dr Killmennie to get in touch with him first.

"I don't know about that, but it's a possibility I suppose, it's certainly something to think about," Colin said.

Lorna had thought of little else over the previous few days, it would mean that all of her dreams would come true.

"Okay. I'll write to Dr Kilmennie – and if that goes well, then we can make further plans and take it from there. It's all in the good Lord's safe hands," Colin said, "He will lead us to the right decision."

"Yes, my love, he will, but it wouldn't do any harm to ask him what's on his mind, would it?" Lorna said.

Colin smiled, "I suppose not sweetheart, but how do you feel about me moving up to Rhua?"

"Oh, Colin, it's like a fairy tale dream come true..."

Just then, and without warning, the pips started to go. "Oh no! I'm running out of coins sweetheart," Lorna said, wishing they could keep talking all night.

"Okay, we can talk about it tomorrow night at 7 and that will give us time to think about where we go from here, how does that sound?"

"Oh Colin, it sounds absolutely wonderful, I love you so much."

"And I love you too. *'Night night, sleep tight…*" Colin said.

"*Watch the midgies don't bite,*" Lorna finished off the children's rhyme.

They both laughed – and the line went dead.

Lorna floated all the way home, she couldn't remember being happier.

Colin was happy too. Knowing that they both wanted the same thing, was very comforting.

Quite unexpectedly, he suddenly felt very tired. All that had happened over the last week or so and the travelling, had taken a lot out of him, and his mind was spinning with thoughts and plans for the future – and so he decided to have an early night.

Moses was curled up on Colin's bed and he lifted him up and said, "Well, my wee friend, it's time for you to go out for the ni..." but before Colin could finish his sentence, Moses jumped out of his arms and went underneath the bed.

He laughed, "So you don't want to go out tonight, eh? Oh well, you can stay in tonight, but just this once."

He made himself a cup of tea, put two custard creams on a plate and went through to his bedroom.

Moses was back on the bed, curled up and looking very comfortable indeed.

Colin got ready for bed humming the lively hymn, *'Standing on the Promises of God.'*

He read a few passages from the Good Book, enjoyed his tea and biscuits and switched off his bedside lamp.

He closed his eyes and whispered, "*Thank you Lord for your unfailing love. Bless Lorna and her family and keep them safe. Thank you for your patience and your guidance – and thank you for watching over me and leading me along the right path. I ask for your blessings upon whatever lies ahead for Lorna and myself. I know that we will be safe in your hands, and with you as our guide, all will be well.*

*I am truly blessed much more than I could ever ask for or ever deserve. Thank you, my loving, faithful God. Amen."*

As he spoke, he felt Moses snuggling in beside him and heard him purring with deep contentment.

Colin closed his eyes and experienced an overwhelming feeling of calm and inner peace, and he knew at that very moment that everything was going to be alright.

He stroked Moses and whispered, "Caidil gu math," (*Cachill gu maa - 'sleep tight/sleep well', something Callum McLeod had taught him*), gave a sigh of contentment and drifted off into a deep sleep with a serene smile on his face and the words of the poet Robert Browning on his lips ~ *'God is in His heaven and all's right with the world'.*

<br>

To be continued….

I hope you enjoyed reading my book and it gave you a smile or two. If you would like to see how Colin and Lorna get on (*spoiler – the Wedding*), with a lot more Highland Hi Jinks along the way, keep a lookout for -

**Book 2** - 'More Tales of a Highland Minister' Continues the exploits of the unsuspecting Minister – and some new characters make an appearance – plus – 'A very Special Day!'

**Book 3**. This is a collection of Short Stories which include ~

*"The Secret Admirer"*
*"The Tinkers Curse"*
*"The Bothan"*
*"The Selkie's Grave"*
*"Gone Fishing" (aka "The Splash Net")*
*"The Black Book of Rhua"*
*"The Banshee"*
*"The Haunted Croft"*
*"The Whisky Olympics" and ~*
*"The Witch's Cat"*

So be sure to keep your eyes open…

# <u>Other titles</u> <u>from this Author</u>

*(so far)*

Tales of a Highland Minister
(Book 1)

More Tales of a Highland Minister
(Book 2)

Even More Tales of a Highland Minister
(Book 3)

*(and others on the horizon)*

These books are all available on Amazon
and Amazon Kindle.

If you enjoyed these stories, could I ask
you to take a few minutes to leave a
review on both Facebook and/or Amazon
so that others may be encouraged to
read and enjoy them too.
Thank you so much.

*Iain*

## Front Cover

*The Old Chapel*
*St John's Scottish Episcopalian Church*
*Ballachulish*
*Scotland*

*(Photo taken by the author)*

ISBN: 978-1-917293-22-8

*I hope you enjoyed reading my book and it gave you a few smiles along the way. Slainte! Iain*

9 781917 293228